Praise for Sanctuaries

"*Sanctuaries* is filled with a variety of strategies that you will want to try immediately! Not only does Dan build the critical case for self-care as a necessity, but he also empowers us to take hold of our time and commitments so we can take action to live more intentionally with healthier mindsets. You will feel like Dan is there coaching you along the way with his humor, personal stories, and authentic insights. Invest in yourself by focusing on the present moment with this text, employ any of the multiple beneficial ideas within it, and live a more full life starting today!"

—Sarah Johnson,
coauthor *Balance Like a Pirate*, teacher, principal,
educational consultant, speaker, and founder In AWE, LLC

"Dan is a true advocate for his fellow teachers and has unique insights about what it means to practice self-care, even when the demands of the classroom feel overwhelming. Dan's practical ideas on mindfulness, rituals, and sanctuaries will give teachers simple steps they can take right now to create change in their lives."

—Angela Watson,
creator of The 40 Hour Teacher Workweek Club
and host of *Truth for Teachers* podcast

"Teachers are consistently listed in the top tier of the most stressful human service professions. *Sanctuaries* provides a holistic and practical relief for helping teachers manage their stress. Read this book, but, most importantly, use the techniques. They work!"

—Dr. Ernie Mendes, PhD,
executive trainer and author of the best-selling books,
Empty the Cup Before You Fill It Up© and *Engage 4 Learning*

"There is a beauty, dare I say a joy, in taking care of others. Servant leadership for educators is organic, and self care should be the same for us—but it isn't. *Sanctuaries* is a blueprint for ensuring that you see the necessity and beauty of taking care of the most important vessel needed to serve from your overflow—your mind, body, and spirit. Dan's heart is on every page, and the practical, easy-to-implement strategies can be done immediately. I recommend you read the book, hug yourself for the investment in your well-being, and buy another one for an educator you love."

—Akilah Ellison,
proud administrator, doctoral student, friend, and mom

Sanctuaries

SELF-CARE SECRETS FOR STRESSED-OUT TEACHERS

Dan Tricarico

Sanctuaries

© 2018 by Dan Tricarico

All rights reserved. No part of this publication may be reproduced in any form or by any electronic or mechanical means, including information storage and retrieval systems, without permission in writing by the publisher, except by a reviewer who may quote brief passages in a review. For information regarding permission, contact the publisher at books@daveburgessconsulting.com.

> This book is available at special discounts when purchased in quantity for use as premiums, promotions, fundraisers, or for educational use. For inquiries and details, contact the publisher at books@daveburgessconsulting.com.

Published by Dave Burgess Consulting, Inc.San Diego, CA
http://daveburgessconsulting.com

Cover Design by Genesis Kohler
Author Photo by Pam Davis
Editing and Interior Design by My Writers' Connection

Library of Congress Control Number: 2018965586
Paperback ISBN: 978-1-949595-12-3
Ebook ISBN: 978-1-949595-13-0

First Printing: December 2018

To John C. Holler

Remember, the entrance door to the sanctuary is inside you.
—Rumi

Contents

Why Is Self-Care Important for Teachers?   i

SANCTUARIES   01
    Intentional and Radical Self-Care   05
    Permission Is Power   09
    Harmony   17
    My Sanctuary Plan
    for Permission and Harmony   22

MINDFULNESS AND MEDITATION   27
    Practicing Mindfulness   29
    Use Your Senses   39
    Find the Detail   43
    Practicing Flow   45
    Meditation   51
    Keep Waking Up   55
    My Sanctuary Plan
    for Mindfulness and Meditation   58

THE FIVE S'S   63
    Silence   65
    Stillness   69
    Subtraction   73
    Space   77

Slowing Down	81
My Sanctuary Plan for the Five S's	86
SELF-CARE	**89**
The Busy Choice	91
Tiny Shifts	97
Your Mental Mix Tape	101
Just One Thing	107
My Sanctuary Plan for Tiny Shifts, Affirmations, and Just One Thing	109
Fast Breaks	111
Rituals	115
Margins	119
Serving	123
My Sanctuary Plan for Fast Breaks, Rituals, Margin, and Serving	128
Pamper Triggers	129
Bliss Stations	133
Soul Food	137
Play	141
My Sanctuary Plan Pamper Triggers, Bliss Stations, Soul Food, and Play	147
Saying Yes	149
Saying No	153
My Sanctuary Plan Saying Yes and Saying No	158

My Sanctuary Plan to Embrace Self-Care	159
RESILIENCE	161
WHAT'S NEXT	167
ACKNOWLEDGMENTS	171
More from Dave Burgess Consulting, Inc.	175
About the Author	179

Why Is Self-Care Important for Teachers?

When my wife and I met for the first time, she said, "You're one of the most relaxed people I've ever seen."

Fast forward ten years and that wasn't true anymore.

I was married, had a mortgage, was raising two kids, and was over a decade into my teaching career.

By that point, I felt much more anxious and stressed about everything.

Ten more years of life (and mounting stress) passed. Our family was dealing with serious health problems, my marriage was going through a rough patch, and the education profession had gone a little nutty. The Testing Machine was out of control, class sizes were enormous (I had forty students in nearly every class), and the budget for supplies and materials was miniscule. It seemed that, year by year, we received less and less support from our administration, the district, and the state.

During that time, I watched some of the most excellent teachers around me melt down, burnout, and leave the profession. In my department alone, we lost three teachers within the space of a couple years. One day, a good teacher friend of mine asked me to cover her class while she spent the period sobbing in the bathroom. At the end of the year, she transferred to another school where she now serves as the librarian. The good news is that she ultimately found a way to cope and is much happier. Another woman walked out one day and called in the next morning to say she wasn't coming in. We never saw her again.

Finally, one of the greatest teachers I've ever known put himself in a situation where he had to be escorted from the classroom. Six years later, he died of a heart attack at the age of forty-nine. To be fair, he had his own personal demons, but I also know he was a visionary. I believe he saw where education was going, didn't like what he saw, and took the only way out he could see. I miss him to this day, and much of what I do in the classroom is still influenced by his amazing work. Losing him was a blow to education and to the students who would never have him as a teacher. This book is dedicated to him.

Before too long, the time came when I could see myself heading in the same direction as these teachers. Things got so bad, in fact, that I went through a period of clinical depression. I was prescribed Wellbutrin, Zoloft, and Lexipro—none of which helped very much. I did come up with a commercial and slogan for Lexipro, however. Imagine me holding the little brown pill bottle and looking into the camera, saying in my best broadcaster voice:

"Life blow? (dramatic pause) Lexipro!"

But in all seriousness, with the world crashing down around my colleagues and me, I thought, "I can't do this. I have ten more years. I have to stick it out. I have to find some way to keep my sanity and make it to retirement."

Changing careers wasn't an option. For one thing, I wasn't even sure I had any other marketable skills. I was over fifty, and I knew I wasn't going back to school to become a doctor or a lawyer, so I had to find a way to make it work. More importantly, I've loved every minute of teaching, and I didn't want to stop.

At a loss for what to do and where to turn, my mind wandered back to my days as a drama major and acting student. Our professors taught us that actors needed to be in a state of "relaxed preparedness," meaning that you were calm, but ready to go; you were relaxed, but ready to perform. To get into that state of being, we did all of these funky breathing, relaxation, and meditation exercises.

I always joke that I do five shows a day. As educators, we are always "on." Creating a state of relaxed preparedness was exactly what I needed. I'd also been interested in Zen, Eastern philosophy, and mindfulness, so applying this approach of meditation and purposeful relaxation to my teaching practice suddenly seemed like a good fit.

I started a blog called *The Zen Teacher* about how to use these techniques. Honestly, the blog started as a way for me to write down some reminders for myself, but when I promoted the blog, teachers responded to the message. Realizing then that others might benefit from this approach, I wrote a book called *The Zen Teacher: Creating Focus, Simplicity, and Tranquility in the Classroom*, which covered how to be relaxed and prepared and ready to perform. My timing was pretty good because mindfulness was just emerging as a technique to use in education. Like actors, teachers are significantly more effective when they are relaxed, present in the moment, not preoccupied with the past or the future, and ready to perform.

The truth is, I am still not as relaxed as the day I met my wife, but since writing *The Zen Teacher* and practicing its concepts, I definitely feel calmer and happier than I have for the past two decades, and I'm much less worried about how I will "survive" my job and make it to retirement. In the process of becoming a "Zen teacher," I've learned a few more things about myself, this profession, and how we can all experience life and teaching from a happier, less-stressed, more peaceful state. And as with my previous book, that state begins with a focus on self-care—something educators tend to neglect. If *The Zen Teacher* reminds you to take care of yourself, *Sanctuaries* shows you how.

You've heard the saying, "You can't pour from an empty cup." Well, teachers are such beautiful people, such givers and servers, that they completely empty their cup and then, if it will help a student, colleague, or a member of their own family, they will gladly hand over the cup as well.

Your well-being and the success of your students, relies, in many ways, on your ability to thrive—not simply survive.

In this book, you will learn why you need to take back your cup. Your well-being and the success of your students, relies, in many ways, on your ability to thrive—not simply survive. In the pages that follow, I'll share practices and strategies for relaxation, mindfulness, and self-care that will equip you to experience life from a place of relaxed preparedness, mindfulness, and strength. While we're at it, I want to show you how to fill your cup with the things you love so you can give more without depleting your resources.

A sanctuary is a place of rest and refuge, of safety and sanity, and often of the sacred and the holy. While there is no objective, absolute answer to what a sanctuary is, we can discover what that word means to us through some simple practices and strategies. To that end, I have included activities throughout the book to help you do just that.

These activities—think of them as rest and reflection stops in your reading—are labeled "My Sanctuary Plan," and each one can help you figure out what your definition of a sanctuary is, as well as develop what one (or many) might look like for you. Because this culture does not value stillness, reflection, or self-care, you must learn that the answers and approaches will not, and cannot, be decided by others. They can only be defined by you. It's important to remember, as the poet Rumi said, that the "entrance door to your sanctuary is inside you."

If you read this book carefully and apply what you learn, maybe I can provide you with one or two of the keys that can help you unlock that entrance door.

Once you pass through the threshold, the rest is up to you.

Sanctuaries

Where do you go to heal, to rejuvenate, to lick your wounds when life has been unkind? How do you go about creating a feeling of wholeness and erase the overwhelming notion that The Universe is out to get you? What do you do to cultivate the sense that, at the end of the day, things will ultimately turn out all right?

In other words, where is your sanctuary?

A sanctuary, according to Merriam-Webster.com, is "a place of refuge and protection." It is a kind of shelter that might be a literal place—a church, for example, or a park, or a mountaintop, or the ocean, or your house, or maybe even the classroom where you teach.

But that shelter could also be figurative, a protection against someone else's rage or abuse or a shelter against an overwhelming personal sense of sadness, frustration, or fatigue. In that case, perhaps, your sanctuary is a state of mind that arises from experiences you have—praying, listening to music, or spending time with loved ones.

Given the stressors of modern American education, it is crucial that we, especially as classroom teachers in the trenches, have a place to retreat. We need to access and develop that sense of calm and equanimity that allows us to regroup and come back to our work lives refreshed and ready to go another round with the challenges that life and education throw at us.

People in all walks of education need to take care of themselves so that they are able not only to survive, but thrive in the classroom. We must learn to create the conditions where our mental, emotional, and spiritual healing and rejuvenation is valued and looked after, so that we all make it through to retirement—or whatever our life may hold after we leave our schools and classrooms.

Years ago, I read a book called *The Courage to Teach: Exploring the Inner Landscape of a Teacher's Life* by Parker Palmer, and it changed the focus of my entire career. Palmer gave me permission to teach from the perspective of "who I am" and to see teaching as a path and a struggle and a grand experiment. Even when that experiment doesn't go perfectly, if my heart and mind are in the right place, my teaching practice will always make a difference for my students who, like us, exist in a largely indifferent world. In short, Palmer helped me turn my classroom into one of my sanctuaries.

Palmer, who is now a columnist for a site called *On Being*, recently wrote a post discussing the importance of sanctuaries. True to Palmer's form, the entire column was inspiring, but the following quote resonated with me particularly deeply:

> Today … in a world that's both astonishingly beautiful and horrifically cruel, "sanctuary" is as vital as breathing to me. Sometimes I find it in churches, monasteries, and other sites designated as sacred. But more often I find it in places sacred to my soul: in the natural world, in the company of a trustworthy friend, in solitary or shared silence, in the ambience of a good poem or good music.[1]

What matters most is not what or where our sanctuary is, but that we have one.

What Palmer tells us here is that what matters most is not what or where our sanctuary is, but that we have one. It is our own realization that we have a sanctuary and how it helps us create a sense of focus, simplicity, and tranquility that ultimately saves us. Our sanctuary becomes a safe haven when life confounds, a sacred space where we can find stillness, silence, peace, and contentment when we are pushed to our limits.

The truth is, life is too difficult, too challenging, too full of pain and grief and violence to not find a place where we can rest and heal and grow. We so often need a respite from the world where we can find a way to deal with the chaos and confusion. All of us will face troubled times, so it is imperative that we find a place of protection so that these troubled times do not consume us. We are too important, too special, too loved—even if we think otherwise—for that to ever happen.

So if you look around and don't see a place or a situation where you feel safe and secure and can wrap a blanket of warmth and love around you, either make it a priority to find one or ask for help from someone you trust because everyone needs—*in fact, everyone deserves*—a sanctuary.

Where will you find yours?

List three places, life approaches, or mindsets that are your sanctuaries in day-to-day life:

1. _____

2. _____

3. _____

Intentional and Radical Self-Care

The world can be a big and scary place; stress is inevitable. The way we navigate that stress determines the difference between thriving and burning out. In a profession that has historically ignored the need for self-care, we must find ways to cope with the tension and anxiety and deal with the stressors inherent in our work. Because, ultimately, the responsibility for taking care of ourselves lies within our own hands.

If we don't make the choice—and it *is* a choice—to take care of ourselves and value our peace of mind and expansiveness of spirit, then it most likely won't happen. Sure, we might experience random and serendipitous moments of relaxation and respite, but stress and workloads often expand when left unchecked. Unfortunately, self-care, though necessary and beneficial, is not something our society rewards; in fact, it often rewards just the opposite. In a world where its inhabitants are addicted to smartphones, laptops, and Netflix accounts, we are responsible for breaking the cycle and stopping to value and honor those times when we recognize our own deep impulses to slow down, breathe, and maybe even meditate. It may seem unorthodox and unconventional to stop the busyness, especially given what our neighbors and colleagues are doing, but making the choice to pause can be critical, even life-saving, especially when those impulses are buried and suffocated by relentless stress.

Honoring and valuing these impulses is something I call *intentional and radical self-care.*

Let me break down those two words for you:

Intentional—Self-care is not going to happen by accident. The word *intentional*, then, means by choice or on purpose. In other words, no one is going to hand it to you or do it for you. You may have an incredible support system of friends and loved ones—and if you do, fantastic—but, chances are, no one in your life is likely to walk up to you, look you in the eye, and say, "You know what? You look pretty worn out. Why don't you take a nap?"

Whether you call it self-love, self-care, or self-compassion, these things don't typically happen as a matter of spontaneity and serendipity. They are skills, muscles and—like all muscles, all skills—they only get stronger and better when exercised and practiced.

Self-care is a choice—your choice. It takes purposeful intention to make it happen. One thing you can do to increase your odds of a little personal TLC is to schedule it on the calendar. Writing something down makes it more real and gives it a little more gravitas than if it remains as a "someday/sometime" idea in your mind.

Radical—Radical means different from what is typical or ordinary. In this Zen teacher's mind, then, radical means unusual, not like we always do it. If you want to break the frenetic auto-pilot pace you slip into and learn to improve your self-care, you have to do things differently than you have been doing them. This is not only a great challenge for us but also for those around us.

I first heard the expression *radical self-care* used by the writer Anne Lamott. She recognized that self-care often broke with some kind of traditional norm. This means that if you insist on time for renewal and rejuvenation, for example, you may face resistance from those around you who are used to you behaving in a certain way. They may experience what is called *role stress*, which is what happens when the role they are accustomed to you playing in their lives changes, and they find themselves feeling uncomfortable or even threatened by the new you. When that happens, your best recourse is to accept what is and proceed with nonjudgment. Intentional and *radical* self-care calls you to set boundaries that value and respect your personal needs and desires even if it pushes you (or someone else) out of a familiar comfort zone.

Lamott tells us that "Radical self-care is what we've been longing for, desperate for, our entire lives—friendship with our own hearts."[2] Isn't the idea of having a friendship with our own hearts a lovely thought? If we cannot commune with ourselves first, then it's just not clear to me how we can best serve or be present with others.

I remember one day, years ago, I was cleaning the house with my family. After I finished some domestic task that made our domicile a little more inhabitable, I made my way downstairs and announced that I was "going to take a break." After this proclamation, I stretched out on the couch in the living room. Upstairs, I could hear a slight increase in the noise of the tasks being accomplished. Things were being done a little more vigorously. Drawers were being shut a bit more aggressively. And as my family members wandered by me on the couch, I could sense the heat of their gaze on me. I imagine they were thinking, "Why do *you* get to take a break when we are we still working our asses off?" And while part of me was hoping, I suppose, to model what it was like to take care of myself in the hopes that my typical Type A family members would realize that a little balance is a helpful perspective, I was smart enough to know I shouldn't actually say, "You can take a break any time you want."

I mean, I didn't have a death wish.

In years past, when I tried to match my family's rhythm of constant forward motion with no breaks, no rest, no Sabbath of any kind, I not only felt unhappy, but I would often watch them push themselves to the *n*th degree and end up sick or worn out or grouchy, simply because they hadn't honored the impulses they were experiencing that encouraged them to take care of themselves.

When I talk about intentional and radical self-care, keep these two points in mind:

1. If you want to treat yourself better (and thereby be in a better position to love, give to, and serve others), you must do it on purpose and by choice.

2. When you do so, your actions will seem atypical or out of the ordinary.

Taking action with purpose and by choice, especially when that action is not considered typical by others, can be a subversive, rebellious act.
So I guarantee you'll ruffle feathers.
And I promise you'll get funny looks.
So what?
Be a rebel.
Value your own needs.
Take care of yourself.
What's the worst that could happen?
Inner peace?

Permission Is Power

When a student turns eighteen, he or she can vote in elections and fight for our country, but just weeks before, that same student was asking you for permission to go to the bathroom.

As any elementary school teacher can tell you, permission is a part of The Education Machine. When it comes time to take one's third-grade class to the local botanical garden or petting zoo, for example, or when the high school teacher is showing an R-rated movie or taking the drama class downtown to see the play with the salty language, the teacher in charge of the field trip must send home a permission slip to be signed by the parents or guardians.

Naturally, the first reason for the permission slip is to say, "If a wild goat mistakes your child's fingers for flesh-colored carrots and your little one loses both pinkies, it's not exactly my fault." And in the fine print, there is a bunch of legalese absolving the teacher, the school, the district, the state, several federal politicians, and my ninety-year-old grandmother of any liability.

For our purposes, though, I am more interested in talking about the second use of the permission slip. Liability aside, the permission slip is used because the parent is ultimately in charge of what the child does and does not do, and the permission slip is the parent's way of saying, "Yes, it's okay with me that this is happening."

As adults, however, the time comes when, magically, we are suddenly in charge of ourselves. As grown-ups, no one is responsible for the permission over us, but us. Some might argue, perhaps justifiably, that by entering into a number of different types of relationships—marriage, parenthood, etc.—we concede being fully in charge of ourselves and instead share that authority with another. Even if that is accurate to some degree, we can still give ourselves permission to choose, permission to be happy, permission to start or end a relationship, permission to make more money, permission to take a risk or to take action. What we do with our lives is entirely up to us.

What an awesome (and wholly terrifying) proposition!

The control and responsibility we have over our existence means that we are the only ones who can give ourselves permission for self-care and self-compassion. It also means that we must find the strength to give ourselves permission to slow down, rest, or pamper ourselves in a way that helps us avoid burning out, melting down, or crashing altogether.

Giving ourselves permission for such things isn't always easy. As the saying goes, *It's easier to ask for forgiveness than permission*—even when we're asking *ourselves* for that permission. As someone who, for years, needed a great deal of help in learning to be more assertive, I get it. For many of us, giving ourselves permission to take an action that we think will inconvenience others feels close to impossible. Sometimes we have to force ourselves to look out for number one, to take the bull by the horns, throw caution to the wind, and put ourselves first by granting ourselves the permission for, dare I say it? Self-love.

Because, say it with me, "Self-Care *is* Self-Love."

Like many of the ideas in this book, giving ourselves permission for self-care is a path and a practice, and there will be stumbling, steps back, and misjudgments. First, remember to give yourself permission to forgive yourself for those missteps. If you are acting in sincerity and generosity, there isn't any reason you shouldn't have that forgiveness.

As teachers, we want to continue giving and giving and giving—to everyone but ourselves. Time and time again, I've heard teachers (including myself) say things like, "I don't deserve that," "I can't afford that," or "That's okay; I'll do it next time." But the irony in that sacrifice is you're not doing anyone any favors, especially yourself.

We live in a world of abundance. Refusing to give yourself permission to participate in self-care or self-compassion is not helping anyone but is, instead, simply hurting you. No one benefits if you deprive yourself of rest, relaxation, or rejuvenation; in fact, you and the ones you're being so careful to take care of are actually served *less* when you are crabby, running on fumes, or in some other way, performing at less than your best. If you really want to help those folks, give yourself permission to rest, thereby insuring that, once you return, you will be at the peak of your skills and performance.

Giving yourself permission is not about being rude, stepping on other people's toes, or becoming one of those people you hate because they feel that they are the glowing, shining center of The Universe. Where self-care is concerned, giving yourself permission is simply about taking the initiative for self-compassion and having the courage to say, "This is something I need right now (a break, a nap, a pedicure, whatever), and it's okay that I do it."

The bottom line is, it's up to us. We can do whatever we decide we want to do, so at what point do we decide that we are worth taking care of?

Giving oneself permission to do anything—to act, to remain passive, to stay on the ledge, to leap into the abyss—is incredibly empowering, and many of us are afraid of the responsibility that power brings. It's scary. It is also kind, and I happen to think that kindness is one of the most powerful forces on the planet.

I'm sure you think of yourself as a kind person. As a kind person, you love, respect, and take care of those people with whom you want to retain a healthy, positive, and loving relationship.

You give yourself permission to treat them well, don't you?

So why would you do anything less for yourself?

Start now. Give yourself permission to start taking care of *you*. Start this minute, in fact. And then practice by doing it again tomorrow.

And the next day.

Do it because you love yourself.

And because you deserve it.

Permission Slips

In her book *Rising Strong: How the Ability to Reset Transforms the Way We*

Live, Love, Parent, and Lead, noted storyteller and shame researcher Brené Brown talks about the importance of giving ourselves actual, physical permission slips. She tells the story of writing her first self-permission slip on a sticky note before recording a television episode with Oprah Winfrey. She wrote, "When I go on *The Oprah Winfrey Show*, I give myself permission to be excited, have fun, and be goofy." Talk about grace under pressure. If someone told me I was going to record a television show with Oprah Winfrey, I wouldn't need a permission slip because my head would explode!

Imagine the freedom and liberation of giving yourself permission to enjoy life, no matter the circumstances. Now imagine the import and significance of having that freedom and liberation—*that permission*—in writing. In our culture, a signed slip with a signature is a binding contract that *must* be upheld. Why not use that cultural habit to make sure you get what you need?

On a recent Saturday, my wife seemed to be in a particularly low mood.

"What's wrong?" I asked.

"Oh, nothing, really," she said, sighing loudly. "It's just that I wanted to get a manicure and pedicure this weekend, but I've got so much to do it looks like that's not going to happen."

A few moments later, I jumped on my computer and typed up a permission slip that gave her permission to get a manicure and pedicure that weekend, no matter what else needed to happen.

Scrounging around for something to make it look official, so she would take it more seriously, I found a postage stamp, and I slapped it on the permission slip. This "seal" made it seem like the Very Important Document it was. As soon as I saw her again, I handed her the slip of paper.

And by the end of the weekend, the mani-pedi had happened.

By writing it down, I was able to make the desire real, immediate, and actionable, which is exactly what we need to make things happen for ourselves.

That's the power of the permission slip.

When you write out an actual, physical permission slip, you can give yourself permission to:

- Engage in an activity that will allow you to take care of yourself
- Do something for pleasure that seems frivolous
- Do something you've been putting off
- Feel an emotion you've been avoiding because it seems overwhelming

Remember when you were a kid and you had to tell a friend, "I can't. I'm not allowed to"? It might have been that you weren't allowed to walk to the store ten blocks away in second grade because it was too far away, and you had to cross busy streets, or you weren't allowed to ride in Crazy Uncle Earl's car because he had a habit of running stop signs, or you weren't allowed to go to the party at the kid's house whose parents were out of town because your folks were worried about the nefarious activities and proliferation of questionable substances. Who were the ultimate arbiters of what you "were" and "were not" allowed to do? Your parents, of course. They were the ultimate authority.

But now, there is no "outside" authority.

There's only you.

And you have 100 percent authority to give yourself permission to do anything you want, any time you want. I'm not talking about shirking responsibilities or ignoring obligations. I'm also not talking about doing donuts in the faculty parking lot or making come hither looks at the principal's wife at the holiday party. I'm talking about making your own needs and preferences a priority in your life so that they are not stomped on by friends, loved ones, or peers at your workplace.

When you give yourself permission to do something, it liberates you from guilt, doubt, and regret. It excuses you from deliberating or second-guessing about the significance or importance of your choice. By permitting an activity, a choice, or a behavior—especially when it is in writing and when it becomes an actual, living object—*you are saying you believe in yourself and your choices about what matters to you.*

Here is a template for a boilerplate, permission slip. Feel free to modify as needed:

I, [YOUR NAME HERE], give myself permission to

_____ on _____ for _____ (length of time).

_____
Signature

Here is an example:

I, Brad Pitt, give myself permission to read for pleasure from 8:30–9:00 p.m. on Friday night no matter what else comes up.

Brad Pitt

To be wholly effective, the permission slip must be as specific as possible in terms of what exact self-care activity you want to take part in, how long you will do it, and even where, if that's a meaningful part of the process or behavior.

Writing it down gets it out of your head and makes it real. And one of the first steps toward making self-care happen is to see it happening outside of yourself—to see it as part of the natural order of things.

A hard copy permission slip makes doing what's in your heart an intentional act, and doing what's in your heart is a key component of self-care. Before you even get to creating the permission slip, though, you have to have a clear idea of what those things are and create a vivid picture of what doing the act or feeling the emotion would look like. Once you've done that, writing it all out gives it weight and gravity. It makes it real.

Some of us, though, have been going full speed for so long and have kept ourselves so relentlessly busy that, once we finally do stop for a moment of self-care, we have no idea how we should take care of ourselves. One early step is to consider starting a "wish list" of self-care possibilities, activities, strategies, approaches, and events that will soothe and comfort you. If you're not accustomed to giving yourself permission, a "wish list" may be exactly what you need. Then once you pick one of the possibilities on your new list, write your permission slip and, as Captain Picard used to say on the U.S.S. Enterprise, "Make it so."

By creating a permission slip, not only are you avoiding negative results in your life but also signaling to the world what your priorities are and asserting your values. You are stepping into your beliefs of what is important and showing people, through action and behavior, what matters to you.

In short, a written permission slip is a contract with yourself.

Make it real.

Write it down.

Hold yourself to it.

Harmony

When I started working with teachers on their self-care, I talked a lot about achieving a work/life balance. I wanted to show teachers how to reduce their stress, so they could make it to retirement without burning out or keeling over. The end goal was to maximize performance without sacrificing self.

I still want those things for teachers, but I have to admit that, recently, I significantly altered my perception of work/life balance. The shift in my perspective occurred after I read an article where a writer argued that it wasn't work/life balance that was important, but harmony.

In simple terms, *harmony* is the idea that all the parts are working together in a way that is satisfying, complete, and pleasant. In music, for example, harmony occurs when all of the notes and chords blend seamlessly together. In a painting, an eye-pleasing color palette creates visual harmony.

Of course, as much as we may try to adjust the scales to create a balance, life and The Universe frequently have other plans, and we often end up feeling off-kilter rather than balanced. When you seek harmony instead of a precarious sense of balance, however, you can work in alignment with your true self, and in so doing, access a sense of peace and tranquility, even in those moments when the world spins just a little too fast.

When life seems unendingly chaotic and overwhelming, I feel a huge sense of frustration at not being where I want to be, not spending enough time in one place or the other—typically, not enough time in the *life* portion and too much time in the *work* portion. During these times of imbalance, I rant, I rave, and I generally annoy everyone around me, especially my loved ones. These experiences are not even in the same zip code as *balance*, let alone on the same continent as harmony.

Conversely, during times when I feel that things are operating as they should, and my life aligns with my sense of purpose, I experience a sense of flow and harmony. That harmony, I must admit, often feels better—more fulfilling, more peaceful, more pleasant—than simply experiencing a state of balance. It just feels richer and purer in some way.

But things don't always run that smoothly, of course.

Life will always have its moments of busyness, chaos, and unrest. Everyone faces times of stress and anxiety. Thinking in terms of balance can help, but there will most likely never be a time when your life will be 50 percent work and 50 percent fun and relaxation; that vision is unrealistic. What you can do, however, is make choices based on your internal sense of integrity, your value system, and your sense of what's right for you—naturally, organically, authentically—so that you experience a greater sense of peace. In this way, you will create a sense of harmony by tuning into *your* inner rhythms and personal vibrations rather than basing your life on the expectations and obligations of others, which often leads to tension, stress, and anxiety. Especially as a teacher, there are several ways to ensure that you are operating from a place of harmony, even when everything else seems out of balance. Here are a few ideas to help you create harmony in your life:

Know your value system and act within it.

Consistently acting within our value system is what is commonly known as *integrity*. Many of us find ourselves racing from obligation to obligation, adrift, unsure of our priorities, and spending more time trying to put out fires than proactively pursuing the behaviors, actions, decisions, and priorities that are important to *us*.

Sometimes finding what's important in our lives and identifying the foundations of our belief system can be elusive and difficult and, if we're not intentional, can take some of us years to determine. Once we have an inkling of where our values lie, though, and we act within those values, our sense of harmony falls into place with much, much less effort.

Spend time with people you like.

We all know what it's like to be around people who are negative, who drain us, and who drag us down into a pit of cynicism and despair. It's never fun. Thankfully, we can make a mindful choice to change our environment, as well as our level of stress, by simply changing the type of people with whom we surround ourselves. We can choose to spend time with loved ones, good friends, and those who share our goals, our dreams, our rhythms, or our temperament, which can help us achieve harmony and emotional congruence. It's harder, of course, when the negative, cynical people around us *are* our loved ones. In that case, we have some difficult choices in terms of who to keep in our lives. At the very least, we should make a much more concerted and intentional choice to give ourselves the gift of silence, stillness, and alone time. In general, you can also create a greater sense of harmony simply by learning to make yourself one of the people you love being with, even when you're completely alone. Sometimes, especially then.

Listen to your body.

Our bodies tell us more than we think, and we listen to them *less* than we think. If we stop, allow ourselves a few moments of silence and stillness, and then check in with our bodies and truly listen, we can determine what's happening.

Pause for a moment and ask yourself: *Do I need sleep? Am I uncomfortable? Are the stressors I'm experiencing causing physical discomfort like a headache, muscle fatigue, or upset stomach?* Think of your body as a friend, and take some time to check and see what he or she needs. Remember, you can't help a friend with whom you don't communicate.

Practice self-compassion.

If we are aware of our limitations and honor our boundaries, we will experience less stress, simply because we will know when we have overextended ourselves and need to realign our energies toward a greater sense of peace and fulfillment. If we give ourselves permission to carve out time on an overextended calendar for self-care and self-compassion, we will see an increase in our sense of peace and equanimity. Just what the doctor ordered!

Find your Zen practice.

Developing a hobby or practice that fires up our passions and fulfills us mentally, emotionally, and spiritually increases our sense of personal enjoyment and satisfaction. You know those moments when you are so immersed in an activity that you lose track of time? I'm sure you do, and you're not alone. This is your Zen practice.

It's what athletes call being *in the zone*.

It's what scientists call *flow*.

It's what wise teachers call intentional and radical self-care.

Each person's Zen practice will be different. For some, it might be acting or dancing or quilting. For others, it might be hiking or woodworking or singing karaoke. The activity doesn't matter. What matters is that you find an activity you love and that you figure out a way to spend more time there.

Not to put too fine a point on it, but if creating a greater sense of harmony—both inside and outside the classroom—is one of your goals, then choosing (and indulging in) a Zen practice should be one of the great priorities in your life.

Identify your purpose.

When I was growing up, my male relatives were my role models for what life looked like as an adult. Nearly all of them, though, hated their jobs. It seemed that all of them believed that their life choices—forgoing college, having unexpected children early in life, and enduring a whole lot of partying, for example—had locked them into whatever job they were lucky enough to get. I promised myself that my life would be different. Witnessing their everyday misery is one of the reasons I became a teacher: I wanted to love my work, and I do. After much thought and experimentation, I realized that my purpose was to help others and to make a positive impact on the world, and by the time I entered college, I could not think of a more noble way to do just that than by becoming a teacher.

I had identified my purpose and realized a truth about myself—namely, that school had always been one of the places where I have felt my greatest sense of harmony. Even when the stress comes from wondering how I'm going to make ends meet until the end of the month, I still feel totally aligned with my purpose. Sometimes finding harmony is as simple as finding a job or a cause or a calling that is highly aligned with your own inner purpose.

> *Dig deep, listen to what your soul needs to be true to itself, and then act accordingly.*

Dig deep, listen to what your soul needs to be true to itself, and then act accordingly. Even in the throes of endless obligations, even in the face of chaos and anarchy, even when you face intense periods of feeling overwhelmed, you can practice making a choice to be true to yourself. And it does take practice. Living with a sense of harmony, where things are flowing and working, can lead to a greater sense of peace and personal well-being, even when we aren't where we want to be or where we think we should be.

---

[1] Parker J. Palmer, "Seeking Sanctuary in Our Own Sacred Spaces," *OnBeing.org*, September 14, 2016, onbeing.org/blog/seeking-sanctuary-in-our-own-sacred-spaces.
[2] Anne Lamott's Facebook Page. Accessed June 9, 2013. https://www.facebook.com/AnneLamott/posts/it-is-really-not-out-there-whatever-it-is-you-are-looking-for-i-hate-this-sores/332374863558830.

My Sanctuary Plan for Permission and Harmony

Permission

The first key to an effective self-care plan is giving yourself permission. Think of a self-care activity you've been wanting to get to but that you haven't been able to find the time to do. Make sure it's an activity that will renew and fulfill you. Now write a permission slip for that activity. Take it out of your head and make it real! Put it on the calendar. Use the template below any time you want to participate in a self-care activity and want your plan to be real, meaningful, and binding.

Certificate of
PERMISSION

I, [YOUR NAME HERE], give myself permission

to _____ on

_____

for _____ (length of time).

_____
Signature

Harmony

When you choose to participate in activities that are not in alignment with your purpose, desires, and dreams, the result is increased anxiety, stress, and tension. You begrudge the people you're trying to help because your actions do not reflect who you are. I'm not telling you to not help people; what I am asking you to do is be mindful and notice when you've overextended yourself. If your intuition tells you enough is enough, honor that direction and give yourself some time to refill your cup.

In the space below, journal about your belief system and value system. What do you want your life to look like? What are your non-negotiable philosophies? What do you need to say no to? How will you know when you're overextended? What will saying no look like?

Go ahead. Write your script.

Sanctuaries

Sanctuaries

Mindfulness and Meditation

Have you ever driven to work and, upon arriving, realized you don't remember a single moment from the trip? I sure have. It's easy to get lost in the mundane thoughts, responsibilities, and obligations of the day and completely neglect to be present in the moment. But here's the thing: The *present* moment is the only time we are actually living.

Mindfulness is the practice of tuning into the moment and experiencing it without judgment. It's the habit of waking up and being present for what's happening *now*, not spending it worrying about the past or obsessing about the future, but rather fully living in the current moment, which is all we really have.

Practicing Mindfulness

Mindfulness helps us slow down time, take a breath, and increase our sense of focus and peace. It grounds us in the present and helps us experience each moment as we are living it. In short, it helps us be truly alive. Mindfulness is the conscious knowledge that this, *this moment right here*, is the only moment you have, and it is neither good nor bad. It just is. When focused on the past or the future, we lose the gift of the moment in front of us.

How do you practice mindfulness? First of all, you use your senses. The totality of information you receive from the world comes in through your five senses. If you want to "be here now," start asking yourself: What do I see? What do I hear? What do I smell? What do I taste? What do I feel (in a tactile sense, not emotionally)? If you tune into the messages you are receiving from your senses and can experience them as they are, without judgment, you are having a mindful moment and increasing your chances of being fully present.

I once read an article on mindfulness, and the author kept talking about how, if we wanted to be mindful, we needed to "keep waking up." I love the idea that we need to keep waking up because the truth is we are often just sleepwalking through this world, trapped coma-style in the food, electronic device, and media distractions of our lives. It's a rare moment when we wake ourselves to notice the moment before us.

Question: How rich and glorious would our lives be if, a few times a day, we were able to practice our present moment awareness and truly tune in to what was happening?

Answer: We would feel as if we were really and truly living.

How do I know this? My practice over the past several years has proven it. When I take the time to be mindful and wake up to the moment, I feel more alive and more connected to The Universe and everything that is going on around me. It is really quite remarkable.

While we can't stop stress from happening, we can change our response to it when it happens.

This is where mindfulness comes in.

Generally, we multitask, we clump stuff together, we are distracted, fragmented, and unfocused. We fret about the past ("I can't believe that dumb thing I said to Karen!") and worry about the future ("I'll bet that parent phone call I have to make tonight is going to be filled with tension!'). All the while, we are missing the present moment. But life doesn't have to be that way.

We can stop.

Breathe.

Look around.

Use our senses.

Refuse to judge the moment.

Just experience.

Notice what we notice.

Experience the world physically.

Catalogue and acknowledge our experience.

Congratulations! You were just present.

You gave yourself the gift of the *moment*.

From washing your hands to doing the dishes to tying your shoes, any moment you experience during your life can be a mindful moment.

Take folding the towels, for example. Feel your muscles stretch as you reach into the dryer to pull the towels into the laundry basket or feel the heft of the basket as you carry it to your couch. As you lift a towel out of the basket to fold it, breathe in the aroma of cleanliness that is permeating the air around you, and feel the warmth of the towels, fresh from the dryer, on your hands. Be present and experience folding the towels into halves and then into quarters.

My morning view as I drive into work.

Let me share with you a story about mindfulness and my drive to work. I've been a teacher at the same school for over twenty-five years. That means I've made the same commute to and from work nearly seven thousand times. As it happens, I also work in the same town where I grew up. At one point in my drive, the freeway rises up and cuts through two hills. As I emerge on the other side of the summit, I see a glorious vista of the town where I was raised. Some days the town is laid out before me, and I can see the cars zipping by, the sky is blue, and white puffy clouds roll across the sky. Brown and purple mountains look like a Hollywood Matte painting against the horizon. In the winter, thick, gray, cloud banks may cover the blue, and a misty fog might obscure the mountains in the background. Sometimes, if I'm returning to an event at the school after dark, I can see the twinkling of the streetlights as they illuminate the roads and the stars that echo those streetlights in the heavens.

It has actually only been recently—say, within the last few years—that I've really become mindful of this gorgeous view that I am able to experience almost every day. It's just there for the taking, for me to wake up to and enjoy. And sometimes I feel a little queasy when I think of the several thousand times I've driven through that divide in the hills without noticing this God-given gift of beauty because I was focused on my lesson plans, had a meeting to go to, or was rehashing a squabble I had with a family member before leaving for work.

I challenge you: Where along your commute, either to or from work, is there an instance where you can wake up and find some peace and joy and beauty? Pay attention. No matter what your drive looks like, there is a moment, like the one I just described, that you are passing by every day and completely missing.

> *Right here, in the middle of the work I am doing, I am here, and I am present.*

Mindfulness is a Platform 9 and 3/4s-style portal back into living the moments of our lives as they are happening. As I write this book, for example, I am tutoring a young girl who is afraid of the blank page and is freewriting based on some black-and-white, artsy photos I've given her as prompts. I've asked her to use her imagination to tell me the story of what's going on in each photo. As she writes, I tune into my current experience to have a mindful moment: I can hear the birds chirping in the trees outside her kitchen window; some of them sing sweetly, while others petulantly caw and screech. I look out the window and over the backyard fence, and I can see the depths of the canyon beyond their yard and watch as puffs of white clouds do a slow dance across a great expanse of blue sky. Right here, in the middle of the work I am doing, I am here, and I am present. It's a good moment, even though in the back of my mind, I know that my car is leaking oil all over my driveway, and I am wondering how I'm going to cover an unusually high water bill.

You can practice mindfulness in the most mundane moments—even at work, for example. Long before it was The Wizarding World of Harry Potter, there was a place right in the middle of Universal Studios called the Universal Amphitheater. Today young children drink butter beer and stare up in awe at a replica of Hogwarts, but in 1989, when I was in Los Angeles trying to be an actor, the Universal Amphitheater was a concert venue. As a park employee, I was fortunate enough to see many free concerts. Given that this was 1989, that meant performances by such artists as Don Henley, Fine Young Cannibals, and Edie Brickell and New Bohemians.

During the day, I answered phones and typed letters as the receptionist for the Special Events department, the branch of the venue that arranged things such as a trade show for a then-burgeoning computer company called Apple and the auditorium where they taped David Letterman's eighth anniversary special.

I remember one winter night when several of us were working late, and it was already dark outside. I had to deliver something to one of the other receptionists. Like me, Barbara was in her late twenties. She was always nice to me, but she could also be reticent and reserved at times. She didn't smile a lot and was usually all business. I often wondered about her story outside the office because she always seemed to be thinking about something else, and that something else didn't seem to be very pleasant.

That evening, while I waited at her desk for her to sign the paperwork so I could return it to my boss, I happened to look out the window. A beautiful crescent moon hung in the early evening sky, and Venus shone brightly right beside it.

"Look!" I said to Barbara. "Look at the moon. Isn't that beautiful?"

"What?" she said and gave a cursory look to where I was separating the window blinds and pointing.

"And that's Venus," I said, "sitting right next to the moon." I took a moment just to drink it in. "Wow. Isn't that gorgeous?"

"I guess it is," she said and immediately went back to what she was doing.

In the course of my duties, I had to come back to her office ten or fifteen minutes later. As I walked past her desk, she stopped me.

"Danny, wait," she said.

I stopped.

"I just wanted to say thank you," she said, her voice low and her eyes darting around as if she was concerned someone might hear her.

"For what?"

"For showing me the moon," she said. "I wouldn't have seen it, and after you left, I looked at it again. And you were right; it was really gorgeous. So thank you for pointing that out to me."

Not long after, I wrote the following poem, and it's always been a favorite of mine.

Barbara and the Evening Star

Tonight, Venus lies like a wedding stone
Pulled from its setting next to a slice of blue moon.
I rush in, throw open the blinds, and say:
Drink in the beauty, child, as if it was cool wine—
You could use the intoxication, I joke.
But you say nothing.

Later, I wander past your room for no real reason
And your face breaks into a timid smile
Ashamed at your own wonder
And your eyes shine like stars—their radiance
Emitted light years before it reaches me.
"Thank you," you whisper.
"For what?" I ask.
And you point to the sky.
How long I've waited for this night.

I look back now and realize what a mindful moment I was having, long before I was consciously aware that doing so was important or helpful. Furthermore, I realize now what an incredibly mindful act it is to write a poem, given the focus on waking up, emphasizing what's happening right before us, and capturing a certain specificity. It's no wonder I've written poetry since I was eight. Poetry is such an awesome form of written mindfulness. One of the many reasons I love poetry is because it forces us to stop, consider, and focus on the details. It sharpens our experience of the world and is an expression of what it means to "be" in any particular given moment.

Think about what steps you can take to wake up to the world around you, pay attention to what is happening, and experience the present moment. Mindfulness allows you to take just a little segment of your life back and make it your own. When you practice taking back those moments, you will be rewarded—without fail—by feeling more truly alive.

A Basic Exercise in Mindfulness

Because education simply doesn't have enough acronyms, I created something I call "A B.A.S.I.C. Exercise in Mindfulness." I'm hoping this particular educational acronym helps you remember exactly which steps to take when your blood pressure numbers look like the national debt and you're praying you will emerge from your current situation without ending up on the evening news.

When stress rises, practice the following five steps for an increased sense of calm, contentment, and self-care.

Breathe

Stop what you're doing and breathe. Breathe in through your nose and out through your mouth. Slowly. Don't accept the long, gasping inhalations of breath, which are so often a result of increased stress; instead, make it a mindful decision to take slow, soothing breaths where you are connecting to and sensing the rhythm of your own particular breath impulse. Starting with the breath is a key element of any kind of stress reduction behavior or activity.

Acknowledgment

Make it a conscious choice to acknowledge what is happening—without judgment. Simply notice that you are feeling stress, identify the source, ask yourself why it is happening, and, while you are continuing to breathe slowly, isolate how that stress is manifesting itself in your body. Check in with yourself: Do I have a headache? Am I feeling nauseous? Am I clenching my fists? Are my nerves jangling like a mariachi band on crack? At the end of this step, you should have a better idea of where the stress is coming from and how to deal with it; however, it is the next two steps that will move you closer to a sense of peace and serenity.

Sanctuaries

Stillness

Next, in whatever way is possible, create some stillness. Isolate yourself. Sit down. Go into a quiet room. Close your eyes and meditate for a few minutes. Create some silence in a way that allows you to think more clearly.

For those of you saying, "If I had time to do that, I wouldn't be so stressed!" I would argue that this step only takes a minute, and there'll be plenty of stress left for you to wallow in when you're done. But it's important to get still so that the next step in the process can happen more easily and organically.

It's only when you're still that you can truly listen to that little voice inside of you that will guide you in the direction you should go.

Intuition

After finding a way to be still and silent, go deep inside and listen to what your intuition is saying. What is your "hunch" or gut reaction telling you about what is causing the stress and what needs to be done? Do you need to drop the class? Take a nap? Move grade levels? Dump the loser boyfriend (The answer to that is pretty much always yes, by the way.)? By listening to your intuition, you can get clear on what is troubling you in order to make a plan for it to go away—either literally or figuratively.

Your subconscious almost always knows exactly what needs to happen in any given situation, and it's almost always trying to tell you. The trick is listening. Intuition never screams; you need to get still and silent in order to hear its whisper. Listening to your intuition in a state of silence and stillness—and, depending on your faith system, a state of prayer—is a great way to figure out how to deal with the increased stress and find some peace. Intuition always knows True North, and it always tries to guide you there.

But we're not quite done yet. One final step will take us full circle in this mindfulness exercise.

Compassion

After you take some time to breathe, to acknowledge where you are and what is happening, to be still and find silence, and to listen to your intuition, ask yourself this question: "Who needs my compassion?" Discovering who needs your compassion and giving it can be a powerful, final step to reducing tension, stress, and anxiety. There are two critical places to aim your compassion: others and yourself.

Others—The first place you may need to put your compassion to work is with others. Stress is often caused by others not getting what they want. You may not always be able to resolve their issues by providing what they lack, but simply recognizing that another person is also struggling creates empathy. Empathy can empower you to be able to serve that person in a way that reduces stress for both of you. This may, at times, include some kind of forgiveness on your part, especially if you feel slighted or betrayed in some way. A bonus to following all of the steps in this process is that even forgiveness becomes easier. Even if you can't fix the other person's problem, sharing your empathy by saying something like "That must be very difficult for you" or "I can tell that you're facing some challenges" can help the person feel listened to and less alone and can also, by extension, ease his or her stress.

Yourself—A second place to practice your compassion—that is often even more important and criminally overlooked—is with *yourself*. You may find it difficult to give yourself compassion, if you think of doing so at all. So here's the challenge: The next time you get to this point in the BASIC mindfulness process, see if the one who needs your immediate and unlimited compassion is YOU. Then choose to be kind to yourself, just as you would to anyone else who needed your help.

When we share our compassion with ourselves and others, it helps increase contentment and reduce stress for everyone. And once stress decreases, we are all better able to cope or, at least, move on. The next time you feel the throat-constricting squeeze of increased stress, begin by sensing the rhythm of your breath impulse, acknowledge what is happening (without judgment), find some silence and stillness to think, access your intuition, and then ask yourself, *Who needs my compassion?*

And don't be surprised if it's you.

Use Your Senses

We receive every scintilla of information from this world through our eyes, nose, mouth, ears, and fingertips. Everything we know and are expected to interpret and create meaning from comes to us through five separate channels: our senses.

But what if we could use those channels as a tool for self-care?

Years ago, a social science teacher and I were walking through the quad to our respective classrooms, ready to start a new day. As we exchanged pleasantries about the weather, he suddenly smiled, breathed in through his nose, and exhaled with an audible "*ah*." In that moment, he forced me to stop and make myself aware of the gorgeous morning before us: the purple/gray mountains in the distance, the blue sky, the black crows hopping from tree to tree, the white clouds inching across the horizon. After that morning, I began to look at things differently and practice using my breath as a way to tune into my senses and the present moment.

Not long after, I was having lunch with a group of English teachers. While working through his wife's chicken enchiladas, one teacher began describing his lunch in such graphic detail, it bordered on erotica. By the time he got to the last enchilada, I'm sure I was blushing.

These teachers illustrate the importance of using our senses to enjoy the moment. Whether it's breathing in the sweet morning air, enjoying every bite of an exceptional meal, listening to music that moves your soul, or petting a treasured animal after a long day at work, you have the tools you need to find peace in your day. And the best part is, these particular tools are always with you.

We make sense of our world through the ways we experience it, which is why literature teachers often talk to students about the importance of "sensory imagery." We implore our students to ask how a writer is using images in a novel or story that the reader can see, smell, taste, touch, and hear.

Authors are well-versed in the power of vivid sensory detail. In John Steinbeck's touching novel of friendship, dreams, and loneliness, *Of Mice and Men*, the two protagonists, George and Lennie, spend the night in a meadow, just taking a breather, before checking in to a ranch the next morning for some backbreaking work. Steinbeck shows us Lennie as he "dabbled his big paw in the water and wiggled his fingers so the water arose in little splashes; rings widened across the pool to the other side and came back again."

I can see Lennie thrusting his hand in the water and see his "big paw."

I can see the ripples in the creek.

I can hear the splashes.

Writers use our sensory experience to immerse us in *their* worlds.

What if you used yours to immerse yourself in *your* world?

I once wrote a blog post based on one of my own experiences—in this case, breakfast in a diner. This excerpt should give you a sense of how important the senses are in enjoying ourselves and the world:

> *Having breakfast in a diner is one of my favorite things in the world. It probably goes back to those days, right out of college, where my friends and I spent Sunday mornings over a leisurely meal at the local eatery, unconcerned with how long it took or what the rest of the day would require.*
>
> *It was no accident, then, that this morning I ended up at The Broken Yolk, a diner about ten minutes from my house. I was kicking off the beginning of a much needed (and appreciated) day off as our district observed Abraham Lincoln's birthday.*
>
> *The coffee was hot. The eggs, perfectly seasoned. The hash browns? Crispy on the outside, tender on the inside. The sourdough toast was*

golden brown and had just enough grape jelly to give a sweet tang to each buttery nibble. The link sausages were, well, sausage-y.

My goal was to eat mindfully—not in the sense that a two-egg breakfast with sausage, hash browns, toast, and coffee is particularly healthy, but because I was going to enjoy it and decided to be present as I ate it.

I savored the crunchy hash browns and favored the egg whites, while merely sampling the yellow-y yolks. I sipped the steamy coffee slowly and let the rich, full taste dance on my taste buds for a moment before it cascaded down my throat. Spreading the jelly on the toast, it must be said, was a kind of meditative experience. It was an equally conscious choice not to think too much about the ingredients of the sausages, but just to enjoy their textures and flavors.

> *It's the slowing down that makes using your senses a form of self-care.*

To mindfully and consciously use my senses to *really* taste and enjoy every bite, I have to slow down and savor the experience. It's the slowing down that makes using your senses a form of self-care: You are making a choice to be present in the world and to appreciate all of the ways you take in information. When we focus on our senses, we are more likely to experience more peace, appreciation, and gratitude.

A mindfulness exercise called "Take Five" provides guidelines on how to use your senses to refocus on the present and enjoy what's around you. This exercise focuses specifically on three of your senses—sight, sound, and touch—to ground you when you're experiencing stress. The goal is to find your anchor in the moment.

Here is how it works:

Whenever you find yourself feeling stress or an increased sense of tension, stop and "Take Five" by following these three simple steps:

1. Look around and notice five specific things you *see*.
2. Shut your eyes and notice five specific things you *hear*.

3. Tune into your body and notice five things you can *feel*.

The five things you see could be a clock on the wall, a student standing by the pencil sharpener glued to his phone, or even an empty water bottle on the floor by a desk.

The five things you hear could be laughing in the hallways, a truck backing up in the parking lot, or the movie playing in the classroom next door.

The five things you feel could be your arms against your clothing, your bum wiggling on your chair, or your feet squirming in your shoes.

The purpose of the exercise is to use your senses to figure out what your immediate experience is and to "pull you back" into the present moment so that you feel more anchored and less overwhelmed.

Every time you practice this exercise, your experience will be different because your *present moment* will be different. And it's tuning into that different reality that helps you stay grounded and increases your sense of calm because you've come back to where you are.

As you navigate through your world, you'll find plenty of opportunities in your day for obligation and duty. Make it a point to carve out two minutes to use your senses to be in the moment.

See. Hear. Taste. Touch. Smell.

Let your senses help you encounter and enjoy what's right there in front of you.

Find the Detail

In fiction, a specific detail can build credibility and verisimilitude. In comedy, the situational detail can sell the joke, but the *telling* detail sends it into orbit, so it absolutely kills. In poetry, the precision of a detail can be an avenue directly into the heart.

In a classroom lesson, as you know, omitting the proper detail can result in confusion and bewilderment, while including the right one is the stuff of epiphany and revelation.

Details are important. They make a difference. Our goal, then, both as educators and as mindful human beings, is to find the right details and to nurture, celebrate, and, most importantly, recognize and acknowledge them so that we can be present in the moment and use those moments as impetus for our self-care practice.

So often, though, we ignore the details in favor of keeping the machine rolling. But I want to suggest to you that, without seeing the details and being mindful of them, the machine's not worth rolling.

So right now, look around.

Find the detail that defines this moment.

Is it the bird singing outside the window?

The pickle on your sandwich?

The dog snoring in the corner?

Sanctuaries

The crash of the waves at the beach?

The ticking clock in your empty classroom as you prepare for next fall?

The swoosh of the espresso machine at the local coffeehouse?

The humming motor of the air conditioner as it turns on in the family room?

The breeze that tickles the hairs on your arm?

The yellow, pink, and orange buds as they sway on the rosebush outside the kitchen window?

The cheers of the crowd at your daughter's soccer game?

The magical, windchime tringle of her laughter?

Ask yourself: What detail makes this moment...*this* moment?

I know it's easy to let details slip past us, but it's so important to stop now and then to notice them as they happen. In this wacky, chaotic, stressed out, big blue carousel we live on, it is so easy to forget to see those details for what they are—the mosaic of our moments, the patchwork of our days, the comfy quilt of our months and years. When we stop to notice what's going on around us, we can have a better appreciation of the beauty and joy of life's undulations. This simple practice can keep us grounded on what's important and immediate, and that's a form of self-care right there.

Find the detail, and you'll find the moment.

Find the moment, and you'll find the jewel that bedazzles your life.

Practicing Flow

You know what it's like when your lesson is cooking along, the students are engaged, your teaching practice is firing on all cylinders? You know you're in the moment, oblivious to yesterday's problems and tomorrow's concerns. You literally get lost in time.

Most of us would agree that the kind of immersion we're talking about here is one of the joys of the profession. So why don't we seek out that joy and immersion in our "regular" lives? Why aren't we finding ways to practice getting lost in the moment at home, on our own, or during our personal lives as we partake in a joyful activity that we love doing and that fulfills the deepest part of us? And if we did that more often, wouldn't it leave us feeling more peaceful, comforted, and fulfilled?

Coined in the mid-1970s by social psychologist Mihaly Csikszentmihalyi, the term "flow" describes that state of being lost in an activity that you love—one that you get so immersed in that the rest of the world seems to simply melt away. In her article, "Go With the Flow: How States of Blissful Concentration Can Boost Your Overall Health and Well-Being," writer Jessie Scholl says, "Musicians, artists, and athletes cultivate flow states deliberately, whether they're aware of the concept or not."[1]

It doesn't matter what activity you choose, however.

A state of flow is available to all of us.

"It's less about the activity than the relationship between the doer and the thing being done," Scholl says. "If an activity requires some skill, and you love it and are good at it, you can easily lose yourself in it."

And practicing states of flow consistently can have huge health benefits.

As Scholl says later in the article, "Flow triggers the opposite of the fight-or-flight response. Breathing becomes more relaxed, muscles loosen, and heart rate slows. The specific biochemistry associated with flow varies depending on the activity (writing a poem versus going out for a run, for example), but the overall benefits to health and well-being are the same."

So clearly, one of the best ways you can take care of yourself is to find an activity you lose yourself in so thoroughly that you are totally immersed in what you're doing. Imagine all of your obligations and responsibilities melting away, all of your worries, concerns, and fears blurring into the background, and even your problems fading from your immediate focus.

Not bad work if you can get it.

So what can this activity be? Well, anything, really. The funny thing is that you already do it. The problem is that you probably just don't realize what you get out of it, or if you do, you just don't choose to spend enough time there.

Is it a hobby? Sure. But it's more than that. Is it about just taking it easy? Not really. I'm talking about more than binge-watching the latest season of your favorite show on Netflix. Sometimes that's a flow state, but often it's just killing time. What I'm talking about is that activity you think about when you're stressed, that thing you want to get to when the crush is over, that hobby or pastime that lowers your rhythm and reduces your stress because your whole sense of energy, time, and being is focused on that particular action.

Chances are, the activity you're starting to think of when I talk about being "in the zone" even touches you on a spiritual level.

This "in the zone" activity is different for each of us. For me, it's writing. I've been an English teacher for nearly three decades, and as we're leaving for long vacations such as winter break, spring break, or summer, I always tell my students semi-jokingly, "I'm trying to get *to* the exact things you're trying to get away *from*: reading and writing." I tease them about that because reading and writing are my go-to activities when I want to experience the joy of that flow state. I can get totally lost in what I'm writing, look up in an hour or two, and wonder where the time went. But while I am in the moment, I am consumed by tapping the keys on the keyboard and renewing my spirit by creating something (a poem, an essay, or a chapter in this book, for instance) that was not in the world before I made it. During this time, my soul is also engaged, and I'm refilling an empty tank through an activity that is meaningful, powerful, and fulfilling.

For you, the activity might be gardening, working out, surfing, cooking, singing, crocheting, or anything else that allows you to lose yourself in the moment and walk away refreshed and revived. Because being in a flow state creates such peace and rejuvenation, I also call this your Zen practice.

Another way to look at it: This Zen practice activity is also something that, if you don't do it often enough, you get out of sorts, you feel off or not yourself.

This is tragic. And completely fixable.

Let's say, for example, that you know you love to play guitar. Your instrument probably sits in the closet or the corner of the living room, and you pick it up once in a blue moon and noodle around with it for a while, and as you're putting it away, you think, "Wow, that was really fun. I should do that more often."

But you don't.

The next thing you know, months have gone by, the cobwebs have crept around the frets and the tuning keys, your fingers are rusty, and when you do pick up your axe again, it takes a while just to get used to it.

Don't feel bad, though. Most of us operate that way.

But what if we were more intentional about creating opportunities to experience flow?

What if we made a conscious effort to figure out which activity was *the one activity* we wanted in our life on a regular basis, simply because of how it made us feel? And then, what if we chose to go there more often?

How would that change our lives?

How would that change have a ripple effect on all the other areas of our lives, including what happens in our classroom?

That's worth just a little more intentionality, wouldn't you say?

The reason these activities make us feel the way we do is that we are tapping into our authentic selves and are intentionally focusing on our passions, interests, and gifts. We are acting in harmony with our truest personalities and doing what we were sent here to do. *Our job is to figure out how to do it more often.* With intention and practice, this pursuit can be a vehicle for increasing our sense of focus and tranquility.

When we do choose to participate regularly in an activity that renews and rejuvenates us, we will feel more fulfilled and better able to face the other stressors that present themselves because we know we have a place to go, a sanctuary that will help get us through. This oasis is critical for our self-care and overall sense of tranquility.

By now, I'm sure you have a few ideas of what that activity might be. If not, you can start by asking yourself the following three questions:

- What do I love to do?
- What activity makes me feel most in tune with myself, the world, and The Universe?

Once you've identified those activities, ask:

- How can I get to it more often?

You have to be brave enough to carve out time.

Flow state activities do not typically happen on their own.
You have to be brave enough to carve out time.
You have to put it on the calendar.
You have to make it a ritual for yourself.
You must be intentional about acknowledging its value in your life.

Tell yourself you're going to practice your guitar, add a square to that quilt, work on that cabinet you're making in the garage. Be specific: Say, "My flow state activity is cooking, so I'm going to take every Sunday afternoon and lose myself in creating a wonderful meal that I will then share with my friends and loved ones."

Doesn't that sound fun? Wouldn't it improve the quality of your life and renew your spirit knowing that you were continually involved in an activity that brought you joy and caused you to lose track of time?

I promise you that in partaking of that activity, over time, you will discover a greater sense of peace and a heightened focus, energy, and intensity.

Meditation

Carving out even a small amount of time that allows us the indulgence, extravagance, and privilege of focusing on exactly one thing at a time in our multitasking, harried, always-on culture is a truly rebellious act. This, of course, is exactly why I love meditation. By spending a few moments doing nothing, we become calm, centered, and attentive, which enables us to focus and be more productive in every area of life.

The other great thing about meditation is its simplicity. Anyone can do it, anytime, anywhere. You can meditate in the morning when you first wake up, in the evening before you go to bed, in line at the grocery store or bank, even in your car while sitting at a red light. The single prerequisite for meditation is that you have to be breathing, and I would dare say that includes most of us here right now.

Why is breath the cornerstone of meditation? Because the breath is the single most fundamental unit of our existence. If there is no breath, there is no life. So to remember what it is to live, we need to remember to focus on the breath. Breath is not only our life; it is our life *force*.

A Simple Meditation

1. Find a place where you are comfortable.
2. Breathing naturally, begin to focus on the nature of your breath, its impulse and its rhythm.

3. Your eyes may be open or closed, whichever you prefer.
4. Simply direct your attention, your focus, and your mindfulness to the rhythm of your breathing.
5. As thoughts come—*and because you are human, they will*—acknowledge them and allow them to float right through your mind and out the other side without attaching to them, and then simply return your focus to your breath impulse and reconnect with the breath.

I used to think that if I was meditating, I had to completely clear my mind and couldn't have any thoughts at all. This is simply not true. Worrying about eliminating all of my thoughts was a lot of pressure, and it made the idea of meditation much less appealing. Understanding that the point of meditation wasn't to eliminate (or even control) my thoughts liberated me to simply focus on my breath then allow those inevitable thoughts to come and go without interacting with them. When I allowed myself to refocus on the rhythm of my breath and be present, my meditation became a much more enjoyable and successful experience for me.

The bottom line is that meditation is simply a focus on the breath with the purpose of learning to be more fully engaged with the present. As Jiddu Krishnamurti said, "Meditation is not a means to an end. It is both the means and the end."

Three Types of Meditation

One of the myths of meditation is that you have to shave your head, move to the top of a mountain in India, and study with the monks. Not so. You can (I won't stop you!), but you don't have to.

Meditation is an amazingly flexible and adaptive experience.

The truth is: Meditation is an amazingly flexible and adaptive experience. Meditation can be as simple as sitting and focusing on the breath. It doesn't need to be any more complicated than that. I told you anyone could do it. If you want a little more direction, here are some variations that you might find helpful:

1. Gazing—A gazing meditation is when you choose a focal point to concentrate on and use it to focus your breath. This is the kind of meditation they teach you in Lamaze classes when you're going to have a baby. The focal point can be anything—a candle, a picture, a physical object, or even a spot or stain on the wall. Gazing at a fixed point in the distance allows you to concentrate on something so that your focus is laser sharp, and you can reduce distractions.

2. Mantra—If you are a more auditory person, a mantra meditation might be for you. A mantra meditation involves choosing a single word or phrase, or even a sound, and focusing on the repetition of that word, phrase, or sound. In the stereotypical example of a meditation practice, you've probably heard of people meditating to the sound *ohhhmmmm*. That particular sound is used because it is, for many reasons, one of the most universal and fundamental sounds we can make as human beings. But in reality, you can use any word, phrase, or sound that helps you to feel focused, calm, and peaceful. Often, for example, during a meditation session, I inhale on the word "peace" and exhale on the word "tranquility." That works for me. Experiment to find what works for you.

3. Walking—For a very long time, I thought meditating meant sitting in one place and not moving, but this just isn't true. The benefits of a walking meditation include a more relaxed personal rhythm, easier breathing, and soothed muscles. Now I enjoy this form of meditation sometimes more than any other kind. Like the other types, it can be done any time you are on your feet and moving. It works like this: Whenever you want to do a walking meditation, simply focus on your breath, be very mindful of each step you're talking—notice your heels and the balls of your feet touching the ground,

feel your arms swinging slightly back and forth, look around at the sky and your surroundings, and smell the air. One of the reasons I love a walking meditation is that even though you can do it in your living room or bedroom, if you happen to be on a stroll outside (or even walking to and from your car in a parking lot), a walking meditation is an excellent opportunity to get in touch with nature and enjoy and explore your world. If you do a walking meditation on your school campus, it can also help you prepare for work. It's a great practice to start your day off right or to use when you need to take a break and reduce your stress in the middle of the day.

Another myth about meditation is that it takes a lot of time. While it's true that some devotees of meditation visit their local meditation center and do an official sitting meditation called *zazen* for anywhere between twenty minutes to several hours at a time, again, you don't have to. I meditate all the time—in my car, in line at the grocery store, at my desk at work—whenever I want to focus on the moment and practice being a little calmer. But my "formal" meditation practice occurs moments after my alarm goes off each morning and involves setting a three-minute timer on my phone and meditating until the timer goes off.

Just three minutes of sitting and focusing on my breath.

That's it.

And the beautiful part is that everyone can find three minutes in the day to just sit and breathe.

Even you.

Keep Waking Up

Taking time to reflect on what's important can guide us to a better path. But we will never find that path if our noses are constantly pressed against the screens of our phones or buried under a pile of "critical" activities from our to-do lists. It doesn't take much; sometimes contemplation takes the form of simply noticing the beauty around us.

In another chapter, I told you how I started to learn to be mindful during my commute to work. Because I took the time to contemplate what was before me, I not only noticed that the mountains on the horizon were the most gorgeous shade of lavender, but I could also appreciate the soft ring of clouds as they floated through the valley. I basked in the sun as it started spilling onto the streets and glinted off the light posts, radio towers, and store windows. Had I not started thinking about mindfulness earlier that year, I may never have noticed this gorgeous, perfect moment.

The moment I first read the words "keep waking up" in reference to meditation, I knew I had found a new mantra. It was such a great reminder not to take our moment-to-moment existence for granted but, instead, to open our eyes to the glory that surrounds us and to mindfully and consciously express our gratitude.

From then on, I've tried to remember the wisdom in jarring myself from the cultural numbness that comes with living in our society during the twenty-first century. Like most of us, I find myself naturally spending hours of my day glued to my phone, buried in work, vegging out in front of the television, or bingeing on Netflix, but the gift I've given myself, in the last year or so, is the spiritually inspiring, bell-ringing admonition to "keep waking up."

When I remind myself to "keep waking up," it means . . .

- That I notice details around me.
- That I am present with those around me, especially loved ones and those I care about.
- That I recognize the beauty that surrounds me every day, including art, nature, and even manmade beauty, like buildings, airplanes, or city streets.
- That I express gratitude for the simple, ordinary moments in my life when I'm comfortable, safe, and fed.

How do you keep waking up? You need a trigger.

Maybe you have a morning ritual where you stretch or do yoga.

Maybe you sit on the patio with a cup of tea in the evening after a long day.

Maybe you set an alarm on your cell phone that buzzes or gongs or plays Neil Diamond's "Love on the Rocks" to jar you out of your mindless reverie and remind you to wake up to the perfection and promise in every moment. (Maybe your particularly perfect, promising individual moment doesn't involve Neil Diamond's tribute to rocky relationships, but you get my drift.)

You may find yourself "waking up" once or twice a day or even every ten minutes. You may use visual, auditory, or tactile triggers. You may stop for a moment to take a breath, to meditate, or to pray.

How you wake up is up to you.

> *How you wake up is up to you.*
> *That you wake up is critical to your self-care.*

That you wake up is critical to your self-care.

In fact, this idea of "waking up" may be exactly what Aristotle was thinking about when he said, "The ultimate value of life depends on awareness and the power of contemplation rather than mere survival."

Learning to wake yourself up from being in the less-than-conscious, mind-numbing state of unawareness is a form of self-care because it's you taking care of you. Waking up helps you appreciate what's happening, which creates gratitude, which creates joy. When you wake up, you may realize that, *hey, at this moment, I'm relatively well-fed, I have a job that gives me at least some kind of satisfaction, and I have friends and loved ones who care about me, and you know what? That's pretty good.* Things may not be perfect, of course. There may be bumps and hiccups. To that end, waking up can motivate you to do something about those less-than-perfect components of your life so that you fix them, and that is its own form of self-care.

With this practice of waking up, you are giving yourself the gift of the moment and remembering how easy it is to get sidetracked and drugged by the opiate of obligation. Of course, it would be exhausting to be "on" every moment of every day, but the irony is that we must still constantly nudge ourselves into an awareness of what is, to keep waking up to what is happening—so we may cultivate a greater appreciation for what a gift each moment of our lives can be.

Remembering to wake up to the moments in our lives can fill us with a richness and a depth that is not possible when we are speeding through our lives, leaping from obligation to obligation, rushing from meeting to meeting, eating on the fly, and collapsing onto our beds at the end of another day that, in truth, we haven't really lived.

Don't be a zombie.

Keep waking up.

My Sanctuary Plan for Mindfulness and Meditation

Mindfulness

Use Your Senses with the Take Five Exercise

Tuning into your senses is a great way to get connected back to the now. If you want to ground yourself in the present moment and reduce stress by not worrying about the past or obsessing about the future, try this:

1. Sit comfortably.
2. Get in touch with your breath impulse.
3. What are five things you see? (The far wall of your classroom? Trees outside your classroom?)
4. What are five things you hear? (Laughter in the hallways? A plane flying overhead?)
5. What are five things you feel? (How your bottom hits the chair? How your sleeves touch your arm? How your feet land on the floor?)

Find the Detail: What Makes This Moment *This* Moment?

When you feel the stress and tension start to increase and intensify, simply stop, breathe, look around, and find the detail that makes this moment *this* moment. Is it the ornately carved table in the hotel hallway? The palm tree swaying in the early spring breeze? The old man walking across the street against the "Don't Walk" sign? What detail can you identify that will ground you and allow you to focus back on the present moment?

Mindfulness and Meditation

Meditation

A Simple Mantra Meditation

1. Sit comfortably.
2. Get in touch with your breath impulse.
3. Inhale and exhale naturally.
4. Close your eyes and allow them to relax into a soft focus on something in front of you.
5. When you inhale, say or think a simple word, phrase, or sentence like "peace" or "I am content."
6. You can use the same word, phrase, or sentence on the exhalation, or you can use another one; for example, you could inhale on the expression "I am peaceful" and exhale on the expression "I am focused."
7. As uninvited thoughts arrive—and they will—allow them to float on through your mind and, without attaching to them or dwelling on them, simply watch as they pass out the other side of your mind.
8. Inhale and exhale until you feel calmer.

A Quick, Four-Step Breathing Exercise

1. Close your eyes.
2. Inhale for a count of five.
3. Hold for a count of five.
4. Exhale for a count of five.

You can do this breathing exercise any time you feel the stress rising. Repeat as necessary.

Poetry Template

If you have a creative bent or simply love words and written images, try this poetry template. You can write this in a journal, open up a document on your computer, or simply jot it down in a notebook. Whatever works best for you. Especially with an exercise like this, writing is a great way to ground yourself in the present moment and to create a work of art that will serve as a memory of your moment in the future.

Start with:

I see _____

I hear _____

I smell _____

I touch (feel) _____

I taste _____

(These can go in any order, and you may not always "taste" something.)

Then cut out the first two words, revise for clarity and fluidity, change up the order of details, make sure it has a logical progression of ideas (or not, for you avant-garde types), and then you have a poem that documents your present moment. Remember: Your final version may or may not end up with every single detail or image you started with. Finally, if you want to, give it a title.

Here's a sample of what this exercise might look like:

I see the baseball players lined up on the field.

I hear the crack of the bat.

I smell the sweet tang of the barbecued, chicken wings.

I feel the hard, cold, plastic seats of the baseball stadium.

I taste the fizzy carbonation of my Coca-Cola on my tongue.

Once it's revised, you might end up with something like this:

BOTTOM OF THE NINTH

The fizzy carbonation tickles my tongue
As number fifteen steps up to bat.
The cold plastic seats beneath me
Cause my bum to tingle.
Without warning, the bat cracks and,
A nanosecond later,
The ball sails over the fence.
My son rounds the bases.
A homerun!

(It's that simple!)

---

[1] Sholl, Jessie. "Go With the Flow." Experience Life. March 2017. https://experiencelife.com/article/go-with-the-flow-2.

The 5 S's

*I*n the world of self-care, there are five concepts that anyone can practice anywhere, at any time, and they are virtually guaranteed to reduce stress and improve your sense of general tranquility and well-being. Unfortunately, they are probably five of the most ignored concepts in our current culture. Undervalued and under-practiced, these concepts—which I collectively and simply refer to as the 5 S's—are silence, stillness, subtraction, space, and slowing down.

Silence

On any given day, noise abounds.

At school, I hear my students chattering, and the laptop is humming. Someone knocks over a water bottle that slams to the ground with a thud. In the space of three minutes, five kids come up to ask me a question about what we're doing for the day. The jarring shriek of the two-minute "scurry" bell makes me jump. Every. Single. Time. In a class of nearly forty, the frequency of students sneezing creates what sounds like a DayQuil™ symphony gone wrong.

At home, my own children chatter, and the dogs bark. The phone rings. *The Bachelor* drones away on the television. The microwave bell dings; the popcorn is ready! During a commercial, my daughter uses a Dustbuster® to clean up some dirt the dogs have tracked into the house. The piercing sound of the motor goes right through my head.

Our modern world is full of incessant droning, blaring, barking, whirring, and honking stimuli. And it is often overwhelming.

Imagine a break from the world's cacophony.

What we need is more silence. Just a few moments of blessed, lovely silence.

Imagine finding an antidote to the unending onslaught of aural stimulation in our world.

It's there if you want it. But the thing is, no one is going to give you silence. If you want it, you have to take it.

To find silence, we have to make a conscious and intentional choice to remove ourselves from the white noise and immerse ourselves in the healing comfort of soundlessness.

The good news is that you don't need much silence to recharge. You don't have to spend six years in a monastery where all of the monks have taken the same ancient vow of selective mutism. It's much simpler than that. All it really takes is a few minutes of downtime with no other distractions or noise around you. Finding opportunities for silence is easier than you think.

You can find silence:

- If you get up five minutes earlier than everyone else.
- In the car on the way to work.
- In your classroom before your first class.
- In your classroom on your prep period or during recess.
- In your classroom before you go home.
- In the car on the way home.
- Just after dinner.
- Right before you go to bed.

I do private tutoring on evenings and weekends, and it has become my habit to create a little meditative silence by arriving at a client's house about ten minutes early. I park down the street a ways (I have my chosen spots near every client's house), and I use that ten minutes to meditate, pray, run through the lesson in my mind, or just think. That short period of silence is very valuable to me; it is one of my little sanctuaries in life. Sure, I get some funny looks from the Neighborhood Watch people, but in the long run, it's worth it.

What can you do with your silence?

- Pray
- Reflect on your day
- Reflect on life

Silence

- Think more deeply
- Meditate

Why seek out silence?

- It's replenishing.
- It's rejuvenating.
- It can be spiritual.
- It can be life-affirming.
- It can help you tune into your deeper thoughts, inner needs, and intuition.

> *Silence is a critical form of self-care. It soothes and comforts.*

Silence is a critical form of self-care. It soothes and comforts. A few moments of no sound can help you reframe a bumpy day, reboot your attitude about a situation, or help you focus on what's important by eliminating all the other distractions.

In a world filled with a constant barrage of noise, demanding silence is a rebellious act.

But it is also a gift you can give yourself.

If you take nothing else away from this book, I hope you'll hear this . . .

Silence heals.

Stillness

Given the pace of our current culture, stillness might be the one concept in these pages with which we are most unfamiliar. In this hyper-speed, overstimulated world, few of us ever take time to just sit, be silent, and do nothing. And yet, it can be one of the most fulfilling and calming techniques you'll learn from this book.

Somewhere deep in our consciousness, our minds understand the benefit of stillness. Some of us know the profound calm of spending a morning in the mountains listening only to the sounds of nature, others have benefited from a meditative reflection while sitting at the beach, and still others understand the power of silence and stillness during prayer.

Stillness, when done properly, is not only relaxing but spiritual.

It soothes our souls.

As it turns out, you don't have to be in a spiritual location (like the mountains, the beach, or church) to be touched and fulfilled by stillness. You can practice stillness in your home, at your job, or even while parked in your car, waiting for your child to come out of swim practice or dance class. Even though our cultural norms frown on it, stillness is there for the taking. And we have so much to gain from practicing it.

I can hear the argument now: *That sounds great and all, but I just don't have the time to sit still and do nothing; you have no idea how many things are on my to-do list.* I get that you are busy and that stillness seems like a foreign concept, but I'm going to push you to be intentional about making time for stillness anyway.

A Stillness Practice

If you're wondering what stillness looks like, here are some tips for getting started or, rather, for *not* starting and simply being still:

Give yourself permission—The first step in a solid stillness practice is giving yourself permission to have one. It starts by admitting that society's insistence on constant motion, noise, and always being "on" *isn't* the best approach in life—and that you can make other choices. Recognize that you are in charge of changing your circumstances and tell yourself that it is okay to take time to focus on stillness. Permission is a key theme throughout all of the practices mentioned in this book. If *you* don't give yourself permission, who will?

Start small—Long weekends in the mountains spent sitting in a log cabin listening to the trees sounds more like Thoreau than a twenty-first-century educator. It's a good gig if you can get it, but most of us need to start smaller. Can you take five minutes in your day to stop the never-ending hamster wheel of life and simply sit still? Simply take a breath and then spend a moment or two focusing on your breathing? Notice the birds and their songs? Let your rhythm decompress and find just a modicum of peace for just five minutes. For most of us, a stillness practice will start small and grow from there.

Commit—Like all health and wellness routines, a stillness practice will be more effective if it is a part of our priorities and our value system. We have to commit to taking the time to slow our rhythm and be still and have faith that it will improve the quality of our lives. Without that commitment, we simply remain a part of the rat race we are trying to escape.

Do it over time—New and effective habits are not created overnight. Science has shown us that we build new habits by practicing them in manageable chunks over time. The same is true regarding stillness. Being still once for two days and then staying in motion for the next 363 will not give you the life-altering results you seek. Try starting with a smaller goal and finding a set time you can practice stillness every day. Also, remember to give yourself grace when it doesn't go perfectly because sometimes it won't, and that's okay.

When we are still and quiet, we have to focus on what is; and sometimes that's not so pretty.

One of the reasons we avoid practicing stillness is that when we are still and quiet, we have to focus on what *is*; and sometimes that's not so pretty. Subconsciously, we know that if we keep moving and keep making noise, it is easier to avoid the areas of our lives that are disturbing, uncomfortable, causing us inner pain, or simply not working. We know that we should examine and deal with those areas of our lives, but since it is so intimidating or painful, we elect to numb ourselves with the distractions of society—whether that comes in the form of our jobs, our "obligations," or our devices.

Think of those times when you have lain in bed unable to sleep because you were thinking of all of the ways your life was imperfect, all of the things you hadn't done, and all of the disappointments you'd faced. Stillness combined with silence can be painful, so it's no wonder we avoid it by falling asleep watching television or listening to music.

But there's an easy solution. If you couple a stillness practice with some form of meditation, you can let those thoughts come in to your mind, acknowledge them, and allow them to flow right out the other side of your brain. Focusing on breathing and knowing that you do not have to attach to negative or painful thoughts empowers you to learn to focus on the present moment and allows you to then choose to experience the positive elements of your life—instead of always being drawn into an unhelpful and stressful obsession over those areas that just aren't working. Then when you're calm and relaxed, you can also see those imperfect areas with more clarity, which gives you a better chance of finding ways to fix them.

It's a win-win situation.

If you're still thinking that you don't have time to practice stillness, you may want to focus on some of the other concepts and strategies in this book first. That might open up just the tiniest window where you feel comfortable enough to take some time to be still.

If you *are* ready to move out of your comfort zone, even the slightest bit, and you want to slow your rhythm and crank back the speed on your world, pick up your smartphone and set a timer for one minute. Everyone can spare one minute.

For that minute, simply stop.

Say nothing. Don't move.

Notice what you notice.

Without judgment.

At first it will drive you crazy.

Eventually, however, you'll get the hang of just being still.

And before long, that single minute might turn into two.

Or ten.

Or sixty.

And then you'll wonder how you ever lived without those precious, rejuvenating moments.

Subtraction

By the time you hold this book in your hands, the iPhone 7 I am currently rocking will seem as antiquated as the expression *rocking*. Eventually, my iPhone 7 will be filed away right between my floppy disks, beeper, and VHS tapes. One day you might even be reading this on your Apple device that not only makes calls, sends texts, streams movies, and buys your movie tickets but also makes you scrambled eggs while it teleports you to Mars.

As of this writing, however, I have an iPhone 7.

It has exactly one button.

While the iPhone, technically speaking, has a touchscreen where any number of apps can be brought to life with a brush of a warm fingertip, sports volume controls, and the sleep/wake switch, the phone itself has only one button. It is called the "home" button.

For all intents and purposes, that's the only button that matters.

If you've ever purchased an iPhone, you'll know that, unlike every other piece of technology on the planet, it is packaged with virtually no instructional manual.

So why was the iPhone designed with only one main button and packaged with no instruction manual?

Because Steve Jobs knew the power of subtraction.

He knew that less was usually better and that we can create a more streamlined, alluring, and profound experience not by *adding* features, bells, and whistles, but by *removing* them. One thing we can learn from Jobs is that a greater sense of simplicity, care, and style is often a matter of elimination.

Some months of the year, some seasons of life, and even some moments of the day are busier than others. The myriad of activities going on in our lives can overwhelm us. The end of the school year, for example, can be an especially exhausting time. So as counterintuitive as it seems, what if we looked those hyper-busy times directly in the eyes and started removing tasks, activities, and have-tos? What if we started subtracting the stuff that we really didn't need, that really didn't fulfill us, and that didn't move us in the direction of reaching our goals?

Our culture promotes the worship of *stuff*. And most people, including myself, spend far too much time, money, and resources, trying to acquire more things that we don't need and won't use. It reminds me of Ed Norton's *Fight Club* character who said, "We buy things we need with money we don't have to impress people we don't like."

Why do we do this? Mostly, I think, it's conditioning. We see it around us. We're conditioned to buy and acquire. It's what we've learned from our peers; in fact, materialism is part of The American Dream. But it doesn't have to be that way. Henry David Thoreau once said, "The soul grows by subtraction, not addition," which leads me to believe that if the noted Transcendentalist lived in the twenty-first century with its constant need for more, he would have had a heart attack.

We can make a choice to streamline and subtract.

But we can make a choice to streamline and subtract.

When we eliminate, instead of add, we find more time, money, and energy to fill our space and time with activities that fulfill us. The importance of creating the space for our own personal desires and choices cannot be overstated. Subtraction actually opens space for new and better things to come into our lives. And perhaps the most appealing benefit (at least to the lazy part of me)

Subtraction

is that there is simply less to clean and maintain, freeing up our lives for greater and more rejuvenating pursuits.

Be forewarned: If you start eliminating things, you will see that not everyone is comfortable with you embracing the idea of less. Not too long ago, for example, I decided to take everything off my classroom walls. Everything. My plan was to create a blank slate and eventually add decorative touches along the way. But through a combination of busy-ness, lack of any kind of design skills, and the fact that I kind of *enjoyed* the spare, distraction-free, minimalist look of my all-white classroom walls, they stayed bare.

One Monday morning, that all changed. I stepped into the classroom to start my day and felt as if I were in an episode of *The Twilight Zone*. New art hung on my walls—art that I had not put there myself.

Another teacher from my department, who actually did have some design and style sense, sneaked into my room over the weekend and (presumably because he just couldn't take my all-white, blank, canvas walls) hung his art in my heretofore pristine classroom. He had secretly been working on the art in his home workshop and had decorated my room with four pieces total, including a framed picture he had made himself with a couple of our department "in-jokes," an old desktop that he engraved with the pun "Grammar Rules!," and two paintings—one landscape and

One of the only times I've ever been in the woods, literally.

When I said I wanted a "still life" that's not what I meant.

one still life—that he had purchased from a local thrift shop and modified with a picture of Yours Truly that he had hijacked from my social media accounts. In the landscape, I am spying out from behind trees and emerging from the lake in the middle of the painting. In the still life, I'm peeking in from around the corner and popping out of a jug of wine that sits next to a bunch of grapes and a wedge of cheese.

It was a fun gesture, and the pieces are still hanging in my classroom more than two years later (because they are clever and amusing and as good as anything I would come up with personally). But it's interesting to note that at least part of the impetus for his creations was due to the fact that there's something about *less* that gives people the itch to supplement.

Life lesson? Subtraction takes getting used to.

Once you decide that you'll be able to handle the minimalism of subtraction, take a look around and ask yourself:

- Do I really need to buy this thing?
- Where is the excess?
- Where can I streamline?
- Do I really want to clean or maintain one more thing?
- What can I get rid of?
- What can I take off my calendar?
- What don't I need?

Try subtracting from your classroom, from your calendar, from the rooms of your house, and even from your mind. Letting go of negative, unproductive, or outdated thought patterns and mindsets is an amazingly liberating form of subtraction that opens up The Universe to let in all kinds of new, good stuff.

Subtraction is one of the super powers of self-care and provides you with the breathing room that reduces stress, maximizes performance, and increases your sense of well-being and serenity.

Start to win by losing something.

Space

Space can declutter our lives and give us room to grow and thrive. Without the proper amount of space in our calendars, our physical environments, and even our minds, however, we tend to feel boxed in by our claustrophobic schedules and responsibilities. When that happens, our lives become smaller and our experiences more filled with stress. Like everything else in this book, allowing ourselves a healthy amount of space is a choice.

Space is a necessary element in the pursuit of effective self-care, but carving out space takes courage and intention. In a culture where overscheduling is the expectation and the norm, creating space becomes even more important to our well-being; if we don't allow ourselves unoccupied room and time in our schedule, the world will—without a moment's hesitation—consume every last minute. So like the other aspects of self-care, saving a little mental time and physical space for yourself goes against the rhythm of society.

Mental Space

Are you still fuming over the fight you had with your boss last week? Are you worried about next Tuesday's doctor's appointment? Not sure what exactly that mole on your back is all about? When important issues in your life remain constantly on your mind, they may be taking up vital mental space that can be freed up and used for pursuing your goals, focusing on your leisure time pursuits, or even for creating a plan to solve the pestering problem—all of which will lower your stress and increase your peace. If you feel your mind is overrun with worrisome thoughts, try using some mindfulness or meditation techniques you've learned in this book to keep you grounded in the present moment. Give yourself a break and help your mind focus on the now. Create some mental space, and you may find that creating other kinds of space happens more organically and comes more naturally.

Schedule Space

If your calendar is like mine, there are times during the year when every box is filled and there is no wiggle room to pivot when unexpected events occur. This can cause your stress level to go through the roof. Upcoming chapters in this book, including "Just One Thing," "Margins," and "The Busy Choice," will equip you to remove the less necessary events from your calendar so that you can create some space in your schedule and have a little more breathing room in your life. Read those chapters and then implement what you read! Once there is time on your calendar that has been freed up through practice and intention, you can give those hours and minutes back to yourself as a gift. Then you can devote that time to following your passions or to doing absolutely nothing.

It's totally your call.

Physical Space

We all have physical areas in our lives that could stand a little decluttering and reorganizing. Maybe our office desk keeps getting overrun by books, papers, and knick-knacks, or our classroom file cabinets and cupboards get filled with objects and supplies we may need "someday," or we have a family room where people have to navigate an obstacle course of toys, boxes, or pet accoutrement.

To create some physical space, start by finding one area that needs to be dealt with. Go through the detritus and sort the items into three piles: 1) keep and/or repurpose, 2) throw away, or 3) donate/give away. Make a "maybe" pile if you have to, but when you go through that the next time, you *must* decide how to sort the item. When you're done sorting, clear out the clutter!

Reducing clutter is a small act that can have a big impact, and it's especially effective over time. Here are five tiny shifts you can make to create space in your life when you find yourself overwhelmed with the flotsam and jetsam that comes with being the successful educator you are. Note: These are not intended to be (Read this in your best, reverberating, radio announcer voice.) *giant changes*, but instead should be small, consistent, *slightly out of your typical habit*, ninja moves. I promise they will result in less clutter and more space in your world.

1. Clean your desk—I never used to bother cleaning my desk because I didn't think I had time. As a result, every morning I would come in and start my day buried in the debris of the previous afternoon. Then one day, I started taking the time (And we're really only talking about ten minutes or less.) to straighten my desk and remove everything that didn't absolutely have to be there. It is startling how this small habit has made an impact on my disposition and created the sense of peace I feel when I arrive in the morning and sit down to a clean, uncluttered desk. The effect of this single change cannot be overstated. Start doing this tomorrow.

2. Clean some other space—Find some other space in your classroom that needs tidying up. It can be one of the counters, a corner, or a closet that has become overrun with a heap and jumble of excessive nothingness. Clear it. Clean it. Make it *purty*.

3. Take one thing off your calendar—Look at the current week of your calendar and remove one thing. No, not your doctor's appointment or Grandpa's birthday celebration. Look for things that seem urgent and necessary, but aren't. If you don't go to that third church potluck this year, for example, I promise God will understand.

4. Throw stuff out—I guarantee that you have many clothes, old papers, useless lesson plans in file cabinets, ancient teaching units, and even outdated philosophies that can be tossed. Say good-bye and good riddance! You don't need that stuff. If you haven't used it in the previous school year, you won't. My recommendation is to

start practicing by taking one week and throw away ten things every day. If you throw away seventy items in one week, you should feel a difference in the space you've created.

5. Rid yourself of eClutter—If you're like me, the desktop on your computer is a giant mess. My Google Drive is an abyss of files, folders, and images that, judging from the leftover garbage and noise at night, I'm pretty sure a family of four lives in. So here's my suggestion: Every time you open your laptop or your Google Drive, take five to ten minutes and clear out the eClutter: delete files, create folders, move stuff to the trash, or clear your email inbox. If you don't like working in time increments, pick five things you can deal with today. If you do this, even for a week, you'll be able to breathe more easily and find the things you *do* need in that crazy lair we call cyberspace.

Let's face it: Not all of the stuff in your life is there because you like it or need it. Much of it crowds your mental and physical space because it's always been there and you're familiar with it. So what? Less is better! Jettison it! Committing to less creates space to let in more quality, fun, soul-fulfilling stuff that you like.

If you're feeling overwhelmed and burdened by the chaos and the white noise of modern life, exercise a tiny shift by doing one or more of the five steps mentioned above to create some space and breathing room for a more focused, teaching practice and a more thoughtful, fulfilling life.

Space is freedom—freedom of movement, expansiveness, and range of motion. Space is a blank canvas on which to paint or not, an empty room in which to dance or just sit and relax, an open meadow in which to stroll or nap.

Creating space is one of the most immediate, powerful, and effective methods for taking control of how we live our lives.

Slowing Down

What would happen if you were driving in the fast lane on the freeway and you suddenly decided to lower your speed to twenty-five miles an hour?

The results wouldn't be pretty, would they?

Within seconds, you would be mowed down by cars doing sixty, seventy, or eighty miles an hour. But look at it this way: If you moved into the slow lane because you made a conscious choice to reduce your speed, it would be more appropriate to slow down. By making this choice, you reduce the potential for carnage and tragedy. Sure, it might take you a little longer to get where you're going, but you would increase the chances that you'll get to your destination safely—and you just might enjoy the ride a little bit more.

Slowing down in life works the same way.

It seems counterintuitive, but if you want to reach your larger goals—whether they concern your health, your profession, your fitness, your relationships, or your hobbies—slowing down actually increases your chance of achieving them.

How?

Because if you are blazing through your life, moving a million miles a minute, you are more likely to be rushed, less focused, and more prone to accidents and mistakes that will impede your progress. Going too fast can actually decrease the likelihood that you will reach your destination. Or if you do get there, it may take significantly longer than if you had just plodded along—because you will spend much of your time circling back, doing damage control, and mopping up the messes.

The secret, super power to slowing down is *single-tasking*. Take the time to focus on doing one thing at a time and being present as you do it. With such focus, you will improve the accuracy of execution for the things that you need to do and enjoy them more.

Despite what our culture tells us, multitasking is an illusion. You may *think* you can grade papers, feed the baby, stir the spaghetti, do your Sudoku puzzle, and scroll through Facebook on your phone at the same time and do all of them well. In reality, the effectiveness of one or more of those behaviors will suffer. But if you feed the baby and *then* stir the spaghetti and *then* grade the papers, your stress level has a better chance of going down because you're accomplishing more, and the accuracy and quality of what you're doing increases. You might even discover that you don't really need Sudoku or Facebook *right then*, after all. Perhaps you will enjoy those activities even more later when things have settled down.

I know that some teachers will read that last paragraph and say, "He's crazy. He has no idea how much I have to do." But I'm a teacher and a parent, too, so I get it. You're busy and most of us are running as fast as we can in an effort to do more in less time.

I'm not telling you to stop everything. I'm simply asking you to slow down and do one thing at a time. Single-tasking can (and should) be done. I'm not perfect at it. It's a path. There will be stumbles. But I can say this: I'm always happier and calmer when I make the choice not to multitask.

Single-tasking is the secret weapon for effective teachers.

Remember: Single-tasking is the secret weapon for effective teachers.

In this hyper-speed world, when everything you want to do is moving at the speed of sound, it's hard to slow down. But if you choose to reduce your speed and make it a point to single-task, focusing only on one activity, responsibility, or obligation, you can employ a laser-focused attention that will improve the quality of your end product as well as the fluidity and grace of your life. There is a saying, "How you do anything is how you do everything." Make an intentional decision to ignore our society's pressure to rocket through life and, in so doing, to increase the potential to crush the breakneck speed habits you've created that have led to stress and being overwhelmed. Create a richer, more in-depth experience for yourself simply by slowing down.

If you drove your car at one-hundred miles an hour constantly, not only would it eventually run out of gas, but the damage you would do to the car over time would be costly. The same is true of your mind, body, and spirit. If you are constantly operating at top speed, much like the car, you will run yourself into the ground and damage your body—both inside and out—through illness or fatigue.

Speed works better in small increments.

Take your time.

Redefining FOMO

The Fear of Missing Out, aka FOMO, is the feeling you get when you think your friends are doing something that you are aren't doing—and you are afraid that whatever they're doing is making their lives better and that your life is in some way inferior. The FOMO response is to drop what you're doing and join your friends. In one sense, FOMO is really an addiction to speed and busyness. It's the Anti-Mindfulness. It's all about getting caught up in what you *think* you should be doing based on other people's speed and hyperactivity, instead of being okay being in your own present moment.

But what if we redefined FOMO to mean "Fighting Off More Obligation" or "Focusing On My Order?" What if, rather than joining your friends, you made a conscious choice to say no to more new expectations, to slow down the pace of your life, and to enjoy where you are? What if you made your own list of what was important, prioritized your own needs, desires, and expectations, and then followed through on that list? What then? How would giving up the fear of missing out change or improve your life? How much more focused and relaxed would you be?

See if you can come up with your own definition of FOMO that serves *you*, instead of making you its slave.

Fill in the blanks:

F_____ O_____ M_____ O_____

Often, we don't slow down until we are forced to. We push ourselves until we are running on fumes, and then our bodies give out, we get sick, and we have no choice but to stop, slow down, and take care of ourselves.

But I say don't wait until that moment of crisis when slowing down will be a requirement that's out of your control—and far, far less enjoyable (Being sick is one of the *least* pleasant things I do.) than if you made it an intentional living part of your daily journey.

Another metaphor that might be helpful is to think of your local business. During the hours they aren't open, there is probably a sign in their window that says, "Closed." They will almost certainly be open the next day during regular business hours, and everything will be fine. But imagine if they thought, "If we're open twenty-four hours, we'll make more money." Maybe. But eventually, the extra expense and overhead of electricity, rent, and employee wages could put them out of business, and then they wouldn't be making any money at all.

Consider putting up your own "Closed" sign when you need to slow down, regroup, and take care of yourself. You can open your doors again in the morning.

What does "slowing down" look like in today's 24/7 society? Well, it might look a little different for you than it would for me, but here are a few ideas:

- Spend time unplugged from your devices.
- Find a little solitude.
- Watch less news, especially the constant barrage of negative reports we see and hear on a daily basis, whether on television, the internet, or as notifications right on our phone.
- Do NOT read the comments on the online article or Facebook post. Ever.

- Find quiet time for meditation or prayer.
- Park a little farther away from the store and do a mindful, meditative walk to the entrance.

Some of the benefits of slowing down include the following:

- Feeling more focused
- Feeling more present
- Having a clearer idea of what truly needs to be done and what can wait
- Developing more precise goals
- Creating more reflection time, which translates to a life that's easier to navigate
- Adding on fewer obligations
- Creating less stress
- Developing a greater sense of peace and tranquility

We need to bust the myth that there are "so many other things to do." If you are a busy educator, consider which is more important: getting things done right now or getting things done right.

Look around, explore your schedule, and find places to simply do less and slow the pace of whatever it is that you *are* doing.

Slow is the new fast.

My Sanctuary Plan for the Five S's

1. Find a time in your day when you can be silent and still. Don't worry about carving out hours and hours; five minutes or less is all you need. If you don't have five minutes, try for three. If you don't have three minutes, try three deep breaths. The important part is to stop the hamster wheel treadmill of the *doing* in your life and just be still.

2. Reflect on how the stillness made you feel and, in the space below, spend some time journaling about your thoughts regarding stillness.

- Did you enjoy it?
- Were there any parts that where challenging?
- How did your body feel?
- How did it affect your emotions?

3. Also consider this: How might you move forward with a stillness practice?

_____

_____

_____

_____

_____

_____

_____

_____

_____

_____

_____

The 5 S's

Self-Care

When was the last time you did something you could enter under the category of "self-care"? No, seriously. Stop and think about it. Was it reading for pleasure just before bed? The glass of wine during your Netflix binge? Last Saturday's yoga class? Was it your recent mani-pedi? The "date night" with your significant other last weekend?

Whatever it was, if you're like most educators, it may be more than just a little difficult to actually remember an activity you undertook just to renew and rejuvenate yourself. Some of you won't be able to think of anything at all. But that's about to change.

Self-care is critical if you want to avoid burnout and keep stress at bay. In the next few pages, I'm going to share with you why self-care is so important and how to implement your own self-care practice.

The Busy Choice

In the song "Vienna," Billy Joel warns that burnout is the risk of running at top speed. He sings, "Where's the fire?/What's the hurry about?/You better cool it off/before you burn it out."

Mr. Joel may know what's up, but the rest of us—educators, especially—are a little fuzzier on this subject. These days in American culture, being busy seems to be a greatly desired status symbol. We compete over who can be the busiest, most exhausted, most overburdened, and most overscheduled. To make life even more interesting (and dysfunctional), we play subtle mind games about who can be more chained to his cell phone or tablet.

Think I'm kidding? Ever met with a friend or colleague and had this conversation?

You: I'm so exhausted. I've been running myself ragged today. I had to get the kids to school and then I had a doctor's appointment. And then I had to pick up the stuff from the dry cleaners and get home before the plumber showed up.

Your friend: You think that's bad? I had to take my husband to the airport, pick up my mother's birthday cake, and do it all in an Uber because my car's in the shop.

It's as if we're proud of how stressed out we are and how much we had to do, and we're trying to one-up each other.

What if the conversation went differently? What if you took control over your calendar and made some choices in your life that led to a slightly different outcome?

Your friend: I'm so exhausted. I've been running myself ragged today. I had to pick up those graduation announcements, go grocery shopping, get the kids from school, get Tiffany to piano lessons, and then pick up Seth from soccer practice. What did you do?

You: I saw you at soccer practice when I picked up Austin, but then I went home, I threw together a Cobb salad for dinner, we had family game night, and then I read my romance novel in a nice, hot, bubble bath while I sipped a Cabernet Sauvignon.

That's an entirely different conversation, isn't it?

The thing we don't realize is that being busy is not only a habit; it's a choice. Let that sink in. We *elect* to have our calendars filled to the brim; we choose to be on-the-go 24/7. Sure, if we have a spouse, a family, and a mortgage, there are certain responsibilities (But again, all of those things were, at some point, also a choice, but that's a topic for another book.), but how we order and structure the rest of our lives is completely up to us. But we often act like it isn't. We act as if it's a pre-ordained circumstance, structured by some other "power," and completely out of our control.

It's not.

The first step in being less busy, slowing down, and taking better care of yourself is to create new habits and make new and different choices.

The first step in being less busy, slowing down, and taking better care of yourself is to create new habits and make new and different choices. There are twenty-four hours in a day. There are sixty seconds in each minute. That's not conjecture. It's math. Put another way, everyone has the same amount of time. And you—yes, you—could, *if you so chose*, spend those sixty seconds every minute in a way that made you feel less busy.

So when someone says, "I am so busy; I can't seem to slow down; I have no time," what they are really saying—at least to some degree—is, "I have chosen (either by the job I've accepted or in the decision to have kids or pets or the choice to binge watch *The Office* on Netflix) to paint myself into a corner. Now I'm stuck in an obligation (not to mention, a habit), and I don't know how to get out."

That's what we're all really saying when we say we're *soooo* busy.

Choosing to value, prioritize, and act on the idea of intentional and radical self-care is one antidote to the pandemonium of the modern world. It's a way to cut down on the tumult of life and carve out some space to take care of you. Our modern world with its "convenient" technologies has made it not only attractive but, in many ways, necessary to strap balls and chains to ourselves (with names like Galaxy and iPhone) that make us always on, always accessible, and always distracted. These seemingly important disruptions interrupt the moments in our lives—full of creativity, rejuvenation, and joy—that really matter.

In "The Disease of Being Busy," *On Being* columnist Omid Safi writes:

> *What happened to a world in which we can sit with the people we love so much and have slow conversations about the state of our heart and soul, conversations that slowly unfold, conversations with pregnant pauses and silences that we are in no rush to fill? How did we create a world in which we have more and more and more to do with less time for leisure, less time for reflection, less time for community, less time to just . . . be?*

I'm willing to admit that part of that scenario is the luxury of being young. You probably remember times in college, sitting in the dorm room with friends (For me, it was sitting in Denny's, drinking coffee with my drama major friends and talking about theater.), and spending hours in conversations, sharing your philosophies, hopes, and dreams. But then you got married, kids came along, your career amped up, and now it's all you can do to manage dance recitals and violin lessons along with car repairs and doctors' appointments. Your visits with your spouse can often seem like not much more than strategy sessions and M*A*S*H-style triage.

Okay, if you bring Daphne to the orthodontist and I pick up Nick at play rehearsal, one of us can swing by the grocery store to grab something for dinner, we'll eat, and then have just enough time for homework and working on the church rummage sale before bed.

Synchronize watches...
And... GO!

It's true that life sometimes has to be this way. On the other hand, if you're intentional and deliberate, you can recognize that you do have choices, and you can implement different approaches that give you more freedom, more space, and more breathing room to live.

The tough part of self-care is that you have to be willing to NOT be like everyone else.

And we don't like that.

It makes us feel weird.

Furthermore, in the long run, our busyness may not be getting us anywhere at all. Tim Ferriss, personal development guru and *New York Times* best-selling author of the *4-Hour Workweek: Escape 9-5, Live Anywhere, and Join the New Rich* says, "Indiscriminate activity is a form of laziness." Ferriss' point is that if we barrel through life as activity junkies, mindless of where our time is going, that this is a form of laziness because we are not in control of our clock. We are relinquishing the control of our time and, ultimately, our lives to the schedules and calendars we've created with our own choices. We fritter our time away in a manner that leaves us not only unfulfilled but actually *less* productive.

The first step in stopping this treadmill is to decide now to make mindful choices that are based on what you want to do. You don't have to stay on the busy train where you're hanging on for dear life while the things that matter most to you disappear at the bend in the track. Remember when we talked about slowing down and focusing on quality over quantity? That principle applies here too. Yes, things need to be done: There will always be laundry to fold and school lunches to make and bedsheets to change and kitty litter boxes to scoop, but instead of scheduling our days and nights and weeks from top to bottom, we can create margins of space and time by removing some optional choices, stepping back, and making sure that those events fill our lives with meaning and fulfillment.

Most of us, however, continue on our current path without thinking of how busy we are making our lives, all the while lamenting about how much there always seems to do. We never fully realize, though, that we are the ones in charge of our choices, our actions, and our activities. It's not easy to step off that busy train, but if you pull the cord and dare to take life at a slower pace, you might find yourself enjoying life even more than you thought possible.

Tiny Shifts

We think we need to swing for the bleachers.
Hit a homerun.
Make a big move.
Every. Time.
But grand gestures—although nice when they happen—are rare, and they are not the typical way the average person makes progress.

You've heard of baby steps, right? That expression is serviceable, and in truth, I've come very far through the grace of baby steps. But I've always been bothered by the way that term infantilizes us and makes us feel as if we aren't quite developed enough for the large-scale progress we seek.

Recently, I was introduced to a better term: *tiny shifts*. A consistent commitment to the micro-adjustments in our habits, our behaviors, and actions can get us to where we want to go—even if it takes a while.

In California, where I live, it's the tiny shifts in the tectonic plates that keep my home state from jettisoning itself from the coast and taking a refreshing dip in the Pacific. We benefit from the smaller, frequent modifications and alterations under the earth that keep us from ripping ourselves from the rest of the continent.

Small adjustments, over time, keep us on track for where we want to go in the long term.

But it's the "over time" part that's important.

As author, speaker, and self-help guru in his own right, Simon Sinek says

(I'm paraphrasing here), "If you go to the gym for nine hours in a single day, you won't be in shape. But if you go for twenty minutes over nine days, then you'll be in better shape." [1]

A commitment to the smaller action builds the habit.

You need the time to level up, to grow, to practice, to improve and sometimes, yes, even to rest. A commitment to the smaller action builds the habit.

If you commit to making a small choice that is just barely beyond your comfort zone, you ratchet up a notch. If you make tiny shift after tiny shift, day in, day out, month after month, over a year or so, guess what? You will find yourself in a wildly different place than when you started. And I'm willing to bet where you end up will be far closer to your end goal than you may expect—all without the pressure to make some 'pie-in-the-sky-I'm-gonna-freak-out-look-out-I'm-gonna-lose-my-lunch" move.

Because it's not a . . . [cue dramatic movie trailer music] . . . *big move*.

It's just a tiny shift.

Over and over again.

And it's totally doable.

Take me, for example. As a writer, I totally get tiny shifts because the idea of writing an entire book seems completely overwhelming. Then I remember that I don't have to write an entire book in one sitting. I just have to write a single essay of a few pages. And then another. And then another. Seven to twelve months later, I've done that thirty or forty times and then—*viola!*—I have a book.

I'm not really much of a numbers guy, but I did come up with an equation based on the concept of tiny shifts. It goes like this:

$$TS + T = NH$$

It stands for "Tiny Shifts Plus Time Equals New Habits."

If you commit to a tiny shift and practice it over time, you will internalize the behavior and, after a while (science says about thirty days or so), you will have created a new habit. Why not make those positive new habits intentional and, in our case, based on improved self-care?

Here are some examples:

- Can you clean your desk to create some space?
- Can you say no to a new obligation that threatens to encroach on your free time?
- Can you get up in the morning, not grab for your phone for at least thirty minutes, and spend that time reading, praying, or journaling?
- Can you throw out ten things today to create room for positive gifts to enter your life?

Ask yourself . . .

- *What tiny shifts can I make right now?*
- *How often can I make them?*
- *Where would I like them to take me?*

If you're looking for a more Zen-inspired life, don't aim for the bleachers with every swing. Instead, commit to making tiny shifts today and tomorrow. Sometimes it's the base hits that win the game.

Your Mental Mix Tape

Have you ever accidentally dropped a stack of papers and watched as they flittered to the ground like pieces of oversized confetti? Of course, you have. And if you're like me, you may have launched right into an internal monologue that sounded something like this: *Nice going, Ace. I'm so clumsy. I can't believe how dumb that was.*

Would we speak to someone we loved that way? Probably not. So why is it okay to treat ourselves that way?

And why do we do it day in and day out?

One reason is because our internal tape loops have become habits. The self-messaging we engage in becomes so ingrained that we don't even notice it—and we never, ever question it.

If we're going to make changes in our lives and create new habits, like practicing a greater quality of self-care, we need to change those internal tape loops to something more positive. In short, we need to alter our mindset.

One of the great things about the mix tapes people created in the 70s and 80s was that there was never a song on the tape you didn't like. You could fit up to twenty songs on a two-sided cassette tape (or later, a homemade CD that you "burned"), and you knew that you and your friends would love every tune. Another great thing about those tapes was you would include songs from all kinds of genres back-to-back on the same tape. There might be a hard rock song next to a ballad next to a rap next to a country song. No matter the tempo or the rhythm or the lyrics, each song was one you wanted to hear and helped to create the mood you intended.

Affirmations are the mix tapes of our subconscious.

This is exactly how affirmations work. Affirmations are the mix tapes of our subconscious. They are the words we play on repeat every single day of our lives. Doesn't it make sense, then, to make certain our mix tapes are full of words we like and need to hear?

Many people go through life constantly inundating their subconscious with negative messages. *I'm not smart enough. I'm not pretty enough. I'm not thin enough. I'm not strong enough.* These words play like a mixtape of grating 80s pop songs. When it comes right down to it, is "I'm so clumsy!" or "I never have enough time!" all that different and any less annoying than "Hey Mickey, you're so fine, you're so fine, you blow my mind, hey Mickey"? Or how about "You spin me right round, baby, right round, like a record baby"?

Sure, you can tell yourself positive things over and over and benefit from their optimism and enthusiasm, but an affirmation, when done right, follows an *exact* structure:

- **Start with "I am"**—The goal of an affirmation is to supplant the negative tape loop that has been in your head for a very long time. To do this, it is important that you aim the new message directly to yourself.

- **Use present tense**—In a properly structured affirmation, make sure that you are acting as if the behavior or action in the affirmation is already happening. The best way to do this is to write it in the present tense. Make it a "now" kind of thing.

- **Use an "-ing" word**—Changing your habits and internal messages is an action; consequently, you need a *doing* word, a verb, to make things happen. Words like enjoying, focusing, learning, doing, being, etc. can help you make forward progress.

- **Include a feeling word**—Unless you connect your affirmation to your emotions, all you'll have is a nice idea and some pretty words. Even with the "I am" at the beginning, you might still feel as if you are talking about someone else. But if you connect the essence of the affirmation to what you are feeling inside, you will be motivated to act, and you will know that *you* are the person for whom the idea was intended. Include words like loving, excited, thrilled, motivated, enjoying, etc. to marry the message to your feelings.

- Make it specific—If you write a vague affirmation, your results will be likewise vague. Make sure that what you write is as specific as possible and that, depending on your intention or goal, you include a deadline or date of completion. Include the number of papers you will grade, the date by which you will complete your goal, and the deadline for improving your self-esteem. Whatever it is, put an amount, a calendar date, or a time stamp on it to give yourself a fighting chance to internalize the message.

In his book, *The Success Principles: How to Get from Where You Are to Where You Want to Be,* Jack Canfield recommends adding the phrase "or something better" to the end of your affirmations to allow The Universe space to exceed what your mind and heart can imagine.

And I'm all over that.

Here are some examples to get you started:

- *I am enjoying the extra time I have this weekend.*
- *I am manifesting more time in my schedule to read twice a week for pleasure or something better.*
- *I am excited to be meditating twice a day for five minutes.*

Affirmations create positive vibes in your mind that carry over into your life and rewire your brain to receive and, most importantly, *believe* different messages. At first it may seem silly to be talking about things that aren't happening as if they are, but have faith! Talking about them as if they are so instructs your subconscious that these new habits and actions are important and that it should get busy making them a reality. Repeating your affirmations builds confidence, trust, and faith in your heart and soul.

Here are some other things to keep in mind about affirmations:

- **Say the affirmation out loud**—Speaking your affirmations out loud gives them more power, greater weight, and a stronger, more intense sense of reality.

- **Feel the emotion**—It's one thing to mindlessly repeat a sentence, but it's quite another to tie it into your emotions and ask yourself to feel it deeply in your being. Try to internalize the emotions in your affirmations by feeling them in your heart. Learn to embrace the things you want with every fiber of your being and feel the genuine feelings of having what you want wash over your body and permeate your experience. Otherwise, it's just a sentence.

- **Use your body**—By the same token, if your affirmation stays in your head, it remains simply a thought and, as such, is not getting out into the world. To make your affirmation become part of your reality and make it more viable, you must learn to connect your desires with your body. Raise your hands in victory when you repeat your sentence, pump your fists, say it in the mirror, or even record yourself on your phone. Do whatever it takes to raise your physical energy and connect it to the goal or idea you're attempting to manifest.

  At first, this may seem unorthodox. But it works. In *The Miracle Morning: The Not-So-Obvious Secret Guaranteed to Transform Your Life (Before 8 AM)*, author Hal Elrod tells a story about how he heard his roommate screaming in the shower and wondered if he was okay, until he realized that it was merely his roommate's habit, his method for giving his affirmations power and energy. And you know what? When you have manifested what you want and are living the life of your dreams, who looks silly then? If you want to get what you want, make sure you have a kinesthetic goal.

  Make your move. Literally.

- **Be specific**—You must get clear on what you want out of life. You need to tell The Universe exactly what you're after. You need to be crystal clear. Instead of saying, "I will get in better shape," you need to say, "I am excited and pumped about going to the gym three times this week from two to three in the afternoon or something better." The clearer you can be about what you're after, the more you increase your chances it will happen.

Most of us say we don't have time for self-care and personal well-being. But the truth is, that's just another tape loop in our heads.

If you write affirmations related to your self-care and you practice them regularly, before long you will "magically" find the time, energy, and resources to take care of yourself. In changing your internal message, you can change your actions and create new habits that will eventually leave you wondering how you ever lived without proper self-care.

Just One Thing

When you're feeling particularly overwhelmed, stressed out, or overburdened, try this: Look at the entirety of your calendar—your family obligations (both immediate and extended), your household chores, your teaching units, and even your "fun" activities—and then subtract just one thing.

Take it out.

Remove it.

Subtract it from the equation.

Not five things or twelve things.

Just one thing.

It might be a book club you no longer wish to be a part of, a hobby you've lost interest in, the committee you felt coerced to be on, or the church event you never really wanted to attend in the first place.

Whatever.

Just stop. Say no.

Respect your time and space.

And because your needs matter, insist that others respect them, too.

When you remove that one thing, your schedule will have a hole. The question is, what will you do with the space you've created? You can fill it with something you're passionate about or that fulfills you. You can reflect on what you *do* and *do not* wish to do in your life. You can even use it to do a whole lot of nothing.

And that's okay.

What you fill it with, or *whether* you fill it, is up to you.

The absence of that "just one thing" might possibly give you the breathing room you need in order to create more space in your life, see things more clearly, and discover what's really important to you.

My Sanctuary Plan for Tiny Shifts, Affirmations, and Just One Thing

Tiny Shifts

Pick one small change you wish to make in your self-care practice. Maybe it's spending more time in a hobby you enjoy, creating more opportunities for stillness and silence, or even exercising and eating healthier. Whatever it is, make sure it is a small enough shift that you find it manageable and that you will want to keep doing it. Then be consistent about the follow up. After some time has passed—say, a month or so—that tiny shift will most likely have created a new habit for you (Remember TS + T = NH? *Tiny Shifts* plus *Time* equals *New Habits*.), and then you can incorporate a new tiny shift. If you do that two or three times, just imagine how far you will have come in six months and how much happier you might be with the new habits you've created.

Affirmations

Using the structure provided on pages 102-103, write a one-sentence affirmation on each of the following topics:

- Your teaching practice
- Your primary relationship
- Your finances
- Your self-care
- Your spiritual health

Choose one or two of the affirmations that are most relevant to your life experience at the time and repeat them daily during a period of stillness, silence, meditation, or prayer.

Just One Thing

Create some white space on your calendar by emptying a box or two. We often stick with scheduled activities long after they continue to serve us. So choose something that you've been doing out of habit or an outdated sense of obligation. Be mindful and intentional about the changes you will be making in your schedule.

It might be something like:

- Playing cards with friends once a week
- The church committee
- The PTA meeting
- Watching the same old television reruns just out of habit or lethargy

Whatever you find on your calendar that doesn't fulfill you or rejuvenate you has to go. But don't start slashing that pen across weeks at a time (unless you want to).

Start with Just. One. Thing.

Fast Breaks

Stress is a meanie.

And it lies.

When you're in the throes of it, stress makes you feel as if there is no way out and that this is as good as it's going to get. We find ourselves thinking, "Yes, I'm stressed. But there's no time to do anything about it. This is just how it is."

We continue working with our heads down, putting one foot in front of the other, exhausted, spent, but moving ahead—never really getting a chance to regroup or renew our spirits. Our outside selves tell us that there is no relaxing, no winning, and no dancing. Inside, our deepest selves understand what we need and wonder when the chance to breathe or to simply take a break will come.

And then our inside selves want to smack our outside selves upside the head.

For some people, the only way to truly relax is to fly to the Bahamas and sit on the beach, sipping fruity cocktails, while the locals beat on drums and the sun sinks slowly into the horizon across an expanse of lavender-tinted sea. Other people dream of getting away to find some peace and rest in the mountains, or throwing together a picnic and taking the family to the local park, or maybe catching a ballgame.

Sure, those things are relaxing and really work—if you can manage to get away for an hour, a day, or a weekend. But until you find yourself with that kind of time on your hands, there are other options. I call them Fast Breaks or "The 5/10/15 Exercise."

This activity is all about finding tiny blocks of time in your overburdened, over-scheduled lives where you can stop and hit the "reset" button, all without having to book a flight or trouble a travel agent. No matter how busy or stressed you are, if you are mindful and present, I'm certain you can find five, ten, or fifteen minutes to recharge your batteries and face the day renewed.

Five Minutes

No matter how busy your daily life is, you can carve out five minutes to stop, breathe, and regroup. This might be in the morning when you wake up, in the parking lot of your school before you head into the classroom, just after dinner, or before you go to bed.

You may be thinking, "What relaxation can I possibly find in five minutes? That's a measly three hundred seconds."

The answer is plenty.

One morning I was reading the church newsletter in my classroom, and in one of the articles, our pastor said that we could all carve out five minutes a day just to pray. I got up right then, closed the classroom door, and spent the next five minutes just talking to God.

Your five minutes doesn't have to be prayer. It can be stepping outside to watch the birds, reading a poem, doing some deep, controlled breathing, or listening to a song.

"Riders on the Storm" by The Doors, for example, clocks in at 4:35. Not only would that give you the nearly five minutes to stop and be present, but you'd have twenty-five seconds left over to do whatever else you wanted.

Even a few minutes apart from the work-a-day world can make a meaningful difference in the reduction of your stress level and the peacefulness of your mind.

Ten Minutes

If cultivating a sense of preparation reduces your anxiety and stress, ten minutes is enough to make a to-do list for the day. Although that isn't a bad use of time, what if you gave that ten minutes to yourself?

You could read a short article on self-care, sit on the patio watching the birds, or jot a "thank you" note. The number of ways you can use ten minutes to decrease stress and tension are endless and are limited only by your imagination.

Even on the busiest of days, I've learned that I can afford six hundred seconds that are just for me.

I suspect we all can, if we look ahead and plan a bit.

Fifteen Minutes

During the holidays, the outside of my family's house often looks like the Griswold house in National Lampoon's *Christmas Vacation*. Creating that look, however, can be taxing, both physically and mentally. Last year, after removing the last strand of Christmas lights in January, I pulled out a lawn chair, grabbed a cold 7-Up, and set my phone alarm for fifteen minutes. I had a million other post-holiday obligations and still wasn't even quite finished with the task at hand. But I knew that those tasks would be there when I was done with my fast break and that I would be able to approach them with renewed energy and a more positive attitude.

The best part of that soda-sipping fast break was breathing deeply as I noticed the various shades of blue in the sky. I said a prayer of gratitude for the beauty of the gray and white clouds. I was completely present in the moment and enjoying my break. It was a priceless feeling that I still haven't forgotten.

Eventually the alarm buzzed, but only *then* did I venture to the *other* side of our yard to gather and wrap up the seventy-two extension cords.

What can you do with fifteen minutes?

You can have a cup of coffee and do a Sudoku puzzle, call your mom (depending on the mom), clean your desk, take a walk around the block, or hide in the bathroom on your phone (a suggestion from a friend).

In the end, it's up to you.

Look at it this way: When a pot of boiling soup is left on the stove too long, you turn down the heat for a few minutes to let it settle because you are wise enough to know that if you leave the heat unchecked, eventually it will boil over, and then you'll have a hot, frothy mess to clean up. So you take the time to turn it down because it only takes a few minutes.

Fast breaks work the same way.

A Princess or Carnival cruise? Great. A trip to the Caribbean? Awesome. A romantic weekend in a bed and breakfast? Don't mind if I do. But it turns out that basketball courts aren't the only places where fast breaks can help you win.

Rituals

Ceremonies and rituals comprise some of the most profound moments of our existence. Whether large or small, they are a significant part of life, and whether we realize it or not, we use rituals every day to navigate through our journey on this planet.

Consider a wedding, for example. Each one may be different in overall execution, but most or all of them include some kind of music, a reading or two, flowers, an exchange of vows, and a reception (which will include rituals of its own, including food, more music, and possibly dancing). Although the details vary, the rituals that the couple and their guests participate in create a powerful and meaningful experience, as well as memories that last a lifetime.

Rituals help us stay focused on what matters. They help us create habits and practice routines, ground us spiritually, and increase our chances of originating and maintaining a connection with ourselves, each other, and a sense of what might be outside of our earthly experience. Not too shabby, I think, for simply lighting a candle, repeating a prayer, or singing a song.

If rituals are that important and powerful, why do we not give ourselves permission to develop our own personal self-care rituals on a more consistent basis? Why do we not allow ourselves to create and practice a few routines that are designed exclusively for the rejuvenation of our minds, bodies, and spirits?

Your rituals can come in any shape or form; the only thing that really matters is that they work for you.

The good news is that with just a little conscious effort and choice, you can create meaningful rituals for yourself. Your rituals can come in any shape or form; the only thing that really matters is that they work for you.

Parents of young children quickly learn the benefit of developing rituals at bedtime, bath time, and other critical moments throughout the day. Putting aside the more "spiritual" side of things for a moment, finding some ways to structure what happens with our kids, especially when they're young, lowers stress for everyone because the expectations are clear and everyone knows what's going to happen next. When you know what's coming and can anticipate it, the stress reduces.

Little Rituals

Little rituals can happen every day and make even the smallest moments more pleasant and soothing. Like many folks, I enjoy a nice cup of coffee before I officially start my morning. But sometimes, whether I'm at work or home on the weekends, obligations and distractions can interfere, and before I know it, the coffee in the mug has grown cold.

Not long ago, I saw a meme that describes this debacle:

> How to Make Iced Coffee
> 1. Become a teacher.
> 2. Bring hot coffee to school.
> 3. Start doing a million things.
> 4. Drink it cold.

Perhaps you can relate.

One ritual I observe that allows me to enjoy my coffee is to make sure the first sip is just for me. In other words, when the coffee is done, I pour myself a mug and prep it the way I like it (two sugars and, when possible, hazelnut-flavored creamer). Next, I use my senses to get present. I clear my mind and watch the swirling liquid in the mug. I breathe in the wonderful coffee smell, and then as I sip it, I make sure I use my taste buds to fully enjoy that very first sip because that sip is just for me. Depending on distractions and interruptions, I may not get to enjoy any of the rest of the cup, but that first sip? That baby's just for me.

Don't discount rituals simply because they seem little or simple. Little rituals can also matter on a much deeper and more emotional level. When I was a child, for example, my parents tucked my siblings and me in bed every night. As they did so, they would kiss us goodnight, and then without fail, my father would say, "Good night, God bless you, pleasant dreams, and I love you very, very much." He would say this every single night. Did he miss some nights? I'm sure he did. But he performed this ritual often enough that I remembered it, and when my two daughters were born, I carried it on with them as well. They are now twenty and sixteen, and I have almost never missed a night of saying it. This little ritual, which is now over half a century old, was important to me and is now important to my daughters too. I imagine it may even continue when they have their own children. By the way, one of the most moving experiences of my life was watching my visiting father leaning over to kiss my daughters good night and saying his litany of nighttime blessings to them.

Little rituals matter.

Medium Rituals

Medium-sized rituals can be observed in a number of different configurations. You can create medium-sized rituals based on the day of the week—a Monday afternoon yoga class, for example, or a Sunday morning church service, or happy hour with teacher friends on Friday evening. You can also split your medium-sized rituals into morning, afternoon, and evening. Maybe you have quiet time for praying and reading the Bible in the morning, stopping by the park on the way home from school in the afternoon, having a glass of wine with dinner, or reading for pleasure right before bed.

I'm fortunate; I enjoy the people I work with, especially those in my English department. But sometimes it's necessary to create some medium-sized rituals to ensure that we have time for the collegiality and fellowship that we all seem to enjoy; for example, on most Wednesdays, I have lunch with Mr. Peterson, the teacher who "lives" next door. Our medium-sized ritual gives us a chance to hang out a little, have some conversation, and share some stories. It's something I always look forward to. On Fridays, another handful of teachers come by my room to have lunch for the same reasons; in fact, we sometimes plan mini-potlucks and each bring something—whether it's chips, cheese, or guacamole for an impromptu nacho bar, various dessert offerings, or even the makings for a humble PB&J (Although for that eventuality, one teacher brings a certain type of bread that is soooo good, it's known in our little group as "The Jesus Bread." Talk about communion!). As a department, we've also regularly had lunches at a local Mexican restaurant before the beginning of the school year, pre-winter break holiday staff meetings-slash-luncheons, and even acknowledge one another's birthdays with both planned and impromptu celebrations. Invariably, these medium-sized rituals bring us closer together and give a sense of unity, togetherness, and purpose.

Large Rituals

Large rituals often require a bit more time or money than small and medium rituals. They can include annual summer vacations, Fourth of July weekends at the lake, or extended family dinners and caroling on Christmas Eve. Some of these large rituals, which people often refer to as "traditions," are perhaps a bigger commitment for the calendar or the bank account, but they can go a long way toward nurturing you, renewing your spirit, reducing stress, and bringing you closer to the ones you love.

We tend to associate rituals with holidays—putting up the Christmas tree, eating turkey on Thanksgiving, lighting the Menorah—but there's no reason to wait until then. Every day of our lives offers opportunities for creating deeply profound rituals that fill our spirit, help us find focus, and ultimately improve our lives. And if you can combine a ritual with a sense of gratitude, you're virtually guaranteed a greater sense of peace and contentment.

Margins

At the edge of every sheet of loose-leaf notebook paper is a red line called a margin. It gives the writer a boundary that should not be crossed. The margin says, "Yes, you're cooking along, keep going, that's right, that's how you do it; oh, wait! Stop. Don't go past this line; you don't want to go too far. Going past this line will mess you up."

The margin tells the writer when to stop. It takes care of the writer.

Much like the scribe mentioned above, if we want to take care of ourselves, we need margins. Boundaries. Places at the beginning and the end of the work we are doing where we need to stop, where we can find our moments of rest. For the spiritually inclined, in creating margins, we are, in essence, seeking some kind of Sabbath.

Moments combine to create our lives, and you would think that these moments would be the smallest units of time we experience, but they're not. Just as there is a space in that hesitation between when we inhale and exhale, I've learned that between each moment, there is a tiny space, and if you look closely enough, this space contains the entire universe.

Throughout the day, slight gaps like these exist between our moments where we can find just a sliver of peace, a pause, a nanosecond of tranquility, mindfulness, and even prayer. During these times, we can often re-center ourselves and regain our sense of balance and equanimity. These are also the same blips in the time/space continuum, by the way, where some people imagine those stray lost single socks and Tupperware lids go!

Lately, the "spaces between" for me have looked something like this:

Sanctuaries

- After the alarm goes off in the morning, I sit on the edge of my bed, and I breathe slowly and say a prayer. Only then do I reach for my phone and check my Facebook, Twitter, or email. And I probably shouldn't even do it then.
- When I turn off the water at the end of my morning shower, I set my head against the shower wall and enjoy the feeling of the water cascading off of me (sorry for that image, if you were eating).
- When I get to work and turn off my car's engine, I've learned to resist the temptation to bolt from my car and race to the office. Instead, I sit in the car and breathe, look at the trees, and watch the clouds.
- When I step out of the car, I stand by my car, breathe deeply, and look at the nearby mountains. If I have time, I take a second and watch the tall trees swaying in the breeze.
- When the final bell rings at the end of the day, I often have to race to pick my daughters up at school. Nevertheless, I try to sit in silence and stillness, if only for a second or two, at least long enough to manage a single, mindful breath.
- After making dinner and sitting down to eat, I'm learning to resist the temptation to dive into the food; instead, I try to pause and be in the moment and appreciate the meal I'm about to enjoy. I'm not so good at this yet. (Sometimes this one involves prayer as well; some call it saying "grace.")
- Before I go to bed, I'm learning to not just dive under the covers in a lump of stress and built-up anxiety but to sit on the edge of my bed and take some deep, cleansing breaths before getting under the covers. This mini-rest helps me relax and might also include some prayer.

These margins exemplify the small spaces between your day-to-day moments. And as you can see from my list, one way to "chunk" the margins of your life is to separate them into morning, noon, and night. Or maybe before work and after work. Or maybe week versus weekend. It's up to you. The key to finding the margins, however, is to reflect on your life and figure out the moments between when you can stop, set up a boundary, and have a small respite.

On a larger scale, though, your margins may look like this:

- A bike ride after school on Thursday afternoon when you have fewer obligations.
- Reading for pleasure on a Friday night.
- Taking a hike on a beautiful Sunday afternoon.
- Going to the bagel place for a nosh and a cup of java on the day your school has a late start day because of staff professional development meetings.

Not long ago, I had a private tutoring session scheduled at 10:30 a.m. at a local Starbucks with a student who needed some help with his college English class. Knowing the session was scheduled for 10:30, I arrived around 9:15 to create a margin for myself that would include some slow, deep breathing, reading for pleasure, hot decaf coffee, and a hot buttered croissant.

Sure, the sacrifice was that I had to wake up just a wee bit earlier than I absolutely had to, but the psychological benefits of creating that margin far outweighed the sacrifice. At least it did on that day; other days I may have chosen to snore it up for even just a few more minutes because—guess what?—resting is a kind of margin too. But yesterday, I knew I wanted and needed some time just for me to decompress and indulge in a few moments of intentional and radical self-care.

If you truly want to take better care of yourself, start looking for those spaces between the have-tos in your life and those nanoseconds when you can just stop and be present. I promise you they exist. Each of these spaces between can take only a very few seconds or they can be larger margins of time that you "chunk" out for yourself because you and your rest and rejuvenation are worth it (and you *are*).

Finding the margins in your life for self-care can help you stop feeling imbalanced, rushed, or tense. Instead of racing through, grab a few moments to regroup, reaffirm your priorities, renew your spirit, and rediscover your sense of purpose.

Serving

When teachers think of serving their students, many of them love to tell the starfish story.

The story goes like this:

A man is standing on a beach, surrounded by starfish. Worried for their safety, he begins plucking them off the shore and tossing them back into the ocean.

Eventually, another man comes along and says, "What are you doing?"

The first man says, "I'm saving these starfish by tossing them back into the ocean."

The second man looks around the shore and sees the infinite number of starfish on the sand.

"Are you crazy?" he says. "Why are you wasting your time like that? There are too many of them. How can it possibly make a difference?"

The first man looks down, picks up a starfish, chucks it into the ocean, looks back at the second man and says, "Made a difference to that one."

For most teachers, there are too many students. But these dedicated educators plug away, nonetheless. They work. They strive. They achieve. Just like the man chucking starfish into the sea, they do what they can with the resources at their disposal. As Teddy Roosevelt once said, "Do what you can, where you are, with what you have."

It's no different in other areas of our lives. Sometimes we have the time, energy, and money to do more, and sometimes we must do less. *But we can always do something*. And we must have faith that the rest will take care of itself. But one key to deep self-care is to help others how we can.

Not all of us will start non-profit organizations, donate millions to charity, or get the wing of the new hospital named after us. No matter. We can still make a difference. For me, nothing increases my sense of joy and contentment like giving and serving. As a bonus, I get the deeply satisfying feeling that I'm making a positive difference in the world, no matter how small.

Paul Wargo, one of the vice principals at our school when I started teaching more than twenty-five years ago, was one of the finest educational administrators I've ever worked with. He has long since retired, but during the years that we worked together, he was a mentor. I respected him because he was strong, but fair, disciplined, but compassionate. As a young teacher, I remember looking up to him, and he helped me navigate the often-murky waters of being a newbie public school teacher.

Whether formally or informally, he shared his wisdom with me in a way that helped me gain confidence and efficacy. Paul taught me many lessons about teaching, caring, and classroom management.

But there is one lesson I remember with particular vividness.

One day as I was walking to my classroom, I saw Paul ahead of me in the quad, heading back to the office. Without missing a stride, he bent down, scooped up a piece of trash, and dropped it in the next trash can he passed.

Needless to say, we had groundskeepers and custodians—people whose job it was to make sure they kept the campus clean. And though they were wildly understaffed, they always did a terrific job. I have marveled nearly every day at the park-like atmosphere of our campus and arrive in the parking lot every morning with great gratitude to work at such a beautiful facility.

But in that moment, Paul saw a need and acted on it. It was a small gesture, and I'm sure he was completely unaware that anyone was even watching.

But I *was* watching.

And once again, and for the umpteenth time, he inspired me.

When Paul scooped up that piece of trash and put it in the can, it was clear that he was doing it out of a sense of service to our school and pride in the appearance of our campus. And my thought was, *I can totally do that!* Since that moment, twenty-five years later and counting, if I happen upon a piece of trash lying on the ground that's been left over from break or lunch, I scoop it up and drop it in the nearest trash can. I do what I can, where I am, with what I have. And much like Paul, I have faith that, in some way that may not be immediately clear to me at the time, it will help. It will make a difference.

Perfection is never the goal.

Keep in mind, perfection is never the goal. My giving and serving is far from organized or structured, but I try to keep an eye out for opportunities and for causes I believe in.

So where and how do I focus my giving and serving?

As a teacher I am well-versed in Maslow's Hierarchy of Needs. According to Maslow, people's basic needs must be met before they can grow and thrive in the world; they must have food, clothing, and shelter before they can pursue the next level of safety. From there, they can pursue love and belonging and eventually continue on along his hierarchy in a way that helps them succeed and prosper.

So I start with food. Not only am I a great eater and lover of food myself, but I know that if a student is hungry, he or she cannot achieve or succeed. With that in mind, I keep granola bars and crackers in my classroom file cabinet for my students who, for whatever reason, have not eaten. When I give to charities, it is often to the food bank. During many holiday seasons, my local grocery store has a promotion where they fill brown paper sacks with non-perishable food and will donate the $10 bag of food to local food banks whenever a customer such as myself purchases one.

I buy a bag or two every season because I see food as the most basic necessity of life, and I have faith that if my donation is helping people eat, then they can take it from there; they can, with a full belly, create a colony on Mars, develop a cure for the common cold, or figure out what happened to Jimmy Hoffa. But it starts with getting enough to eat. No matter how you slice it, hunger sucks, so that's always been my number one cause.

Sanctuaries

One of the most joyful moments of giving for me occurred in 2015 during the holiday season. That October, I had achieved a lifelong dream of publishing my first book, and I wanted to show The Universe that I was grateful by giving back. So once I received the first royalty check, I went to the grocery store and grabbed a basket. But this time, instead of merely buying a holiday food bank bag for $10, I went up and down the aisles, dropping things in the basket until the basket was full. After paying for the basket full of non-perishable food, I drove it directly to my church that was having its Thanksgiving food drive and unloaded it all into their food pantry. It was most likely the largest, single act of giving I had ever undertaken.

My initial impulse was to help and feed others, certainly, but to suddenly have the resources to give and serve so freely and with such abandon resulted in a sense of joy and exhilaration so deep and intense that I will remember it for the rest of my life. And if this book is in your hands, rest assured it has happened again.

Teachers, of course, are givers. They give and serve every single day of their careers, and they do it proudly, profoundly, and often unceasingly. All I'm suggesting here is that maybe it's possible to give and serve in an even more conscious and mindful way that not only gives to The Universe but also comes back in the form of self-care—meaning that, in the end, you feel good about yourself, you increase your sense of energy and purpose, and you create a sense of joy that comes from a little selfless giving and serving.

So when you are trying to renew your spirit and increase the satisfaction you feel at having contributed to a more positive world, ask yourself the following question:

With what I have right now, what can I give and how can I serve?

When you ask that question with an open mind and an open heart, you will see a myriad of opportunities staring you in the face for how you can make a difference in the world and affect change simply from where you are. I recently saw a meme that, in terms of taking care of hungry people, spoke directly to my heart. It said, "I saw the starving child and screamed at God, until I realized that the starving child was God screaming at me."

Why is serving self-care? Because even though it seems counterintuitive, sometimes you have to send the vibration out (in time, money, or energy) for it to come back to you in the form of relaxation, peace, resilience, or renewal of spirit.

All the rest is faith.

And that part is not up to you.

My Sanctuary Plan for Fast Breaks, Rituals, Margins, and Serving

Fast Breaks

Look at your daily schedule and identify a handful of times during your day when you can create five, ten, or fifteen minutes for a fast break. Then brainstorm a few activities you can do to decompress, relax, and take care of yourself. Listen to a song, take a walk around the block, meditate or pray, spend time with your children or pets. Even finding a couple of times a day to stop, wake up to what's around you, and be present in the moment can make a massive difference.

Rituals

Create two to three rituals—hourly, daily, weekly—where you focus on self-care habits that you can incorporate into your life. Then commit to participating in those rituals and creating those new habits. Maybe it's indulging in a mani-pedi every other week. Maybe it's reading for pleasure for an hour before you go to bed. Maybe it's taking your family to get the Thai food that you love so much every Saturday night. Whatever rituals you create, make sure they help you feel renewed and rejuvenated. Then commit to rituals that center around both margins and service.

Pamper Triggers

I first remember hearing the expression "trigger" as a psychological buzzword sometime in the middle of 2016. It is used to refer to words, phrases, circumstances, or actions that cause—or trigger—highly negative reactions. When psychological stimuli trip a person's memory or internal tape loop, that person is transported back to a previous memory or trauma, which might include references to various kinds of assault, exposure to racial stereotypes or racist epithets, or the viewing of particularly violent or graphic scenes that "trigger" anxiety, fear, or depression.

I started thinking about the term and the effect of triggers, and I wondered if it were possible to "trigger" something positive instead of something negative. What if instead of causing anxiety or fear or depression, you were able to trigger yourself into feeling joy, happiness, peace, serenity, or contentment?

So I've decided to hijack the term *trigger* from the dark side of psychology and rebuild it so that you can re-envision it as a word with a much more positive connotation.

I want to talk about *pamper triggers*.

Everyone likes to be pampered. Everyone likes to feel comforted, soothed, warm and dry, and taken care of. Why wouldn't we? It's an awesome feeling! But most of us carve out very little time to pamper ourselves. For most of us, pampering becomes a rare, random, and serendipitous way to take care of ourselves and bring ourselves joy—especially for men, who

Sanctuaries

often feel trapped by the gender stereotypes, standards, and expectations of appearing "strong" or "masculine."

We all have those certain, special activities, objects, or places, though, that make us feel comforted, soothed, and cared for. Typically, we partake of these rarely, sparingly, and often, quite guiltily. For some, pampering might mean enjoying a monthly deep tissue massage. For others, it might be having breakfast in bed or splurging on the gourmet Hazelnut-flavored coffee. For still others, it might be overly soft towels or a thick bathrobe with *foofy* slippers that you ease your tootsies into after a hot shower or a luxurious bubble bath. Others might enjoy one of Mom's special homecooked meals—her lasagna or enchiladas or egg rolls or pot roast, for example—that she has lovingly spent the afternoon preparing just for you.

If hearing one or more of those examples of what it means to be pampered caused you to travel back to a specific personal memory or if you felt a physical memory of what it was like to be comforted and soothed, congratulations! You just discovered one of your pamper triggers.

But ask yourself: When was the last time you indulged in that activity? If you're like a lot of other people, you may tell yourself you don't have time. Or that taking a break or spending that money is just plain selfish or self-indulgent. Maybe you tell yourself that you're tough; you can make it through life without needing to be pampered. You may even believe that being pampered is just for "sissies" or "weaklings."

This is common, and it is tragic.

Imagine, for a moment, that your friend gave you a gift on a special occasion. Now imagine unwrapping the gift, seeing what it is, and then handing it back and saying, "I'm sorry. I know you meant this as a gift for me, but I'm going to give it back; I can't accept this. I'm just not worthy of this. Besides, I'm too tough to make use of this; this gift is for 'sissies.'"

Can you imagine how crestfallen your friend would be?

Would you do that to him or her?

Of course not.

First of all, over time we have learned through practice to accept the gift graciously, even if we didn't feel at the moment it was exactly right for us. Refusing a gift would be rude.

So why would you do that to yourself—a person you are supposed to love?

Being pampered is a gift we give ourselves.

Being pampered is a gift we give ourselves. When we identify and embrace our pamper triggers, we can learn to graciously accept that gift, just as we would accept a gift from anyone else.

Consider these questions to uncover what kinds of activities might bring you joy, comfort, or a sense of peace:

- What type of pampering do you particularly enjoy?
- What memories do you have of a time or situation where you were feeling especially soothed, comforted, or taken care of? What were you doing? Who was there?
- Why did *that* particular situation make you feel so good?
- How can you carve out more white space on the calendar to go there again?

Good music, for example, is a pamper trigger for me. One of my favorite ways to decompress is to kick back and listen to some classic rock or the blues. (Even as I write, I am jamming to The Rolling Stones' *Blue and Lonesome* album as it pounds from a Bluetooth speaker next to the kitchen table where I'm typing.) I also love soft, comfy slippers, watching a gorgeous sunset, drinking good coffee, eating good food, and snacking on hot, buttered popcorn. In retrospect, that last sentence sounds a bit like a personal ad, doesn't it?

Let me take a moment and tell you a little bit about the hot, buttered popcorn.

Once, my girlfriend at the time and I decided to go to the movies. As we sat there, waiting for the movie to begin, we were munching on some popcorn. At one point, she looked over at me and said, "Why do you eat popcorn so fast?"

"Well, it's like this," I said. "When I was a child, I had three siblings, all younger than me. Two or three times a week, my father would make popcorn for all of us as we sat and watched television. You had to get in while the getting was good. If I didn't eat it quickly, before long, all that was left were the unpopped kernels."

In the days before hot air poppers and microwave ovens, Dad would pour some oil into one of our pans, measure in some popcorn kernels, and in another pan, melt some butter. Sometimes I still go totally old school and make it that way myself.

What I didn't realize until my girlfriend brought it to my attention, though, was that I had learned to eat popcorn like a crazy person because, with five other people digging into the bowl, if you didn't get in fast, you didn't get your share. But despite the Olympic event nature of my popcorn scarfing, I realize now that sitting there in the living room with my family, grabbing whatever popcorn I could get my hands on, while watching *Welcome Back, Kotter*, *Mork and Mindy*, and *Starsky and Hutch*, was an incredibly comfortable, fun, and soothing time for me. Even now, more than forty years later, hot, buttered popcorn is one of my pamper triggers. It reminds me of a time of being loved, and what's more pampering than that?

In some ways, then, finding your pamper triggers is the art of going back. It's about remembering what you loved when you were younger, when you were happy, when you were engaged in an activity or a behavior that made you feel soothed and comforted.

Finding your pamper triggers, on almost every level you can imagine, is a reunion with a more relaxed, soothed part of yourself.

It's reclaiming your history.

Finding your pamper triggers is, in the end, an act of recovery.

Bliss Stations

When I'm ready to relax, I often sit in an overstuffed chair in our home office. It's a big, brown, comfortable, cozy chair, and I plop down into it to read, write, or listen to music. I keep a few things within arm's reach: my bowl of hot, buttered popcorn, my bullet journal, a stack of soon-to-be-played CDs, or maybe even an amber-colored beverage (might be sparkling apple cider, we don't know).

Joseph Campbell, author of *The Power of Myth*, talked about the importance of a sacred place where you can feel soothed, comforted, and taken care of. Sometimes referred to as a bliss station, it is a place you return to when you're ready to take care of you. Campbell tells us:

> *You must have a room, or a certain hour or so a day, where you don't know what was in the newspapers that morning, you don't know who your friends are, you don't know what you owe anybody, you don't know what anybody owes to you. This is a place where you can simply experience and bring forth what you are and what you might be. This is the place of creative incubation. At first you may find that nothing happens there. But if you have a sacred place and use it, something eventually will happen.*[2]

You may not have a designated spot to unwind from your hectic, stressful day. Perhaps, like so many people, you forget to honor your need for rest, reflection, and rejuvenation. But if you listen to the voice within, I'll bet your body craves a place to recharge and simply remove yourself from the white noise of life.

Sanctuaries

I highly encourage you to create a bliss station of your own as a means to improving the quality of your self-care (without dropping five large on a trip to Europe).

So what does a bliss station look like?

It might be ...

- A place in your garden where you have a table and chairs and sit in the evening to listen to birdsong.
- A prayer shrine in the corner of your living room or family room.
- A corner of the room that has some throw pillows, an area rug, some candles, and a favorite book.
- A breakfast nook where you sit and have a cup of tea by the window.
- An easy chair where you meditate, snooze, or read for pleasure.
- A hot bath with bubbles, soft music, and candles or other mood lighting.
- An hour in the gym every morning.
- A Sunday afternoon at the dog park with your favorite fur baby.
- Any other place or time that is already set where you can feel soothed, comforted, and taken care of.

A bliss station is not the place to pay your bills, fret, worry, or complete other chores that stress you out. It's sacred because it's a place you *only* use and *only* go to when you want to be renewed.

One interesting side note: As Campbell tells us in the first sentence of the quote above, your bliss station can be a "when" as well as a "where." Another important point is that, clearly, your bliss station doesn't have to be expensive or elaborate.

As I shared in my book, *The Zen Teacher*, my father frequently came home from work and removed himself from the stress and hassle of the day by donning his headphones and listening to Joe Cocker, Creedence Clearwater Revival, Wilson Pickett, Percy Sledge, or Doo Wop from the 50s. That was *his* bliss station.

Because we also spent many evenings listening to classic rock and R&B as a family, that activity also became one of *my* bliss stations as well.

> *Chances are, you already have a bliss station, and you just don't know it.*

Chances are, you already have a bliss station, and you just don't know it.

My challenge for you is that if you have one, identify it and then use it. Use it regularly and with abandon. Luxuriate in the experience and the habit of it.

And if you don't have one, make one. Today.

Campbell believed that everyone is entitled to some bliss. Not only do I agree, but I've made it my mission to persuade the world that Campbell was right.

And I'm starting with you.

Soul Food

When I was a child in the 70s, I watched a number of sitcoms that featured African-American characters, shows like *Sanford and Son, Good Times,* and *The Jeffersons.* Watching these shows not only became experiences of quality time for my immediate family, but as I said in the last chapter, my parents and siblings and I would often sit in the living room, hovering around a giant bowl of popcorn watching J.J. yell, "Dyn-o-mite!" or laugh along to Fred Sanford clutching his chest, telling his late wife Elizabeth that he would be joining her soon because it was "the big one."

Viewing those shows was a time of learning and understanding what other families did and how they lived.

These particular shows often made references to something called "soul food." To a twelve-year-old Caucasian boy living in a semi-rural part of San Diego, California, who was raised on a steady diet of pot roast, meatloaf, and mashed potatoes, soul food was a foreign and exotic concept. The best I could glean from these shows was that soul food consisted of such delicacies as black-eyed peas, ham hocks, collard greens, and something called *chitlins,* which, if you Google it, you'll probably wish I hadn't mentioned.

Near as I can make out, those dishes were dubbed soul food because they were familiar. And although they weren't necessarily fancy or complicated, they were prepared with great care by someone you loved and who loved you. That connection and the delicious, familiar tastes made the person partaking of the food feel satisfied, taken care of, and content. In short, soul food makes you feel good.

And that's exactly why soul food is a metaphor for life.

We all need more soul food in our lives.

When I think about soul food, I think about those things that literally feed my soul, renew my spirit, and make me feel satisfied and content. They don't need to cost a lot of money, they don't need to be elaborate, and they don't need to last very long.

When I think about what soul food means in my life, I can talk about a lot of things, but one specific thing almost always comes to mind. When I was fifteen, I had begun to be interested in acting, and I met a tremendous group of friends in a play I did at a local community theater. As anyone who is involved in the theater knows, actors in a show are forced to rely on one another, trust one another, and work so intimately with one another that they often grow extremely close by the end of the show's run. When you're an actor, it's almost as if the regular elements of a friendship intensify and happen at hyperspeed. And so it was with this group.

After the show closed, we all continued to keep in touch; in fact, I am still close with at least two people from that cast, having known them now for over forty years. I remember the times we spent hanging out during our show as some of the most enjoyable and soul-satisfying experiences of my life. When I consider why it is that those particular people and activities come to mind when I think of soul food, one of the reasons is that those times felt incredibly authentic. These friends allowed me to be my true self and accepted me without judgment. That made me happy because I knew I could be myself.

We were teenagers. We didn't have a ton of money. The experiences we had and the things we did and the "trouble" we caused were not elaborate. We never traveled far, and whatever plans we made certainly weren't expensive. There were high school football games, for example, and birthday parties and fast food runs. But the warmest memories, and the ones closest to my heart, were the picnics we went on. When we knew we didn't have a lot of money, but we knew we wanted to spend time together, we would all throw some picnic food in the car and grab an ice chest and go to one of San Diego's gorgeous parks to spend the day together, eating, laughing, talking, and even, in our sillier moments, rolling down the grassy hills together. We once took a picture of the eight or ten of us who were at the picnic at the end of one of these beautiful days, and we were all just one big pile of friends, smiling at the camera, leaning on each other. That picture represents one of the most genuinely and deeply fun experiences of my life. I kept it tucked into the edge of a picture frame on my desk for years.

(L-R), David, Karen, Robin, me, Bucky, Judy, Bobby, and Jamee enjoying ourselves in the park somewhere in the late 70s.

I didn't realize it in the moment, but the people in that group and the days we spent at the park were part of my soul food.

The key questions to ask yourself for this section are . . .

- What is *my* soul food? And,
- How can I spend more time there?

The activities can be simple and cheap. The truth is that if they are genuinely soul food for you, they probably will be. Maybe it's going outside for a breath of fresh air. Maybe it's walking around the block. Maybe it's reading for pleasure. Maybe it's hiking in the hills above your house. Maybe it's visiting your cousins who live in the next town. Of course, I'm using the term "soul food" as a metaphor, but it just as likely could be taken more literally, and your "soul food" might be baking for friends or getting the family around the table for a nice dinner.

Figuring out your soul food is slightly different than your hobby, your Zen practice, or the activities that keep you in a state of flow. It's more about the objects, places, or people (or all three) that fulfill you, make you happy, or bring you closest to your true self. It's not merely an activity but a way of living that you can feel deep inside and that feeds and nourishes you.

When you make a decision to partake of your own, specific, individual soul food, you are sending a message to yourself that you matter, that you are worthy, and that your needs are valuable.

What would your life be like if you did that more?

Play

Growing up, I could often be found wandering the neighborhood with my friends. We would be riding our bikes up and down the streets, or hanging out in front yards, or sitting in rooms talking about Elton John, *Charlie's Angels*, or that cute redhead in third period. There seemed to be a virtually unlimited amount of time to do what we wanted and engage in any activity or sometimes no activity.

And as young people who didn't know any better, we took it entirely for granted.

In "The Busy Trap," journalist and author Tim Krieder talks about a similar upbringing. He says, "I used to do everything from surfing the *World Book Encyclopedia* to making animated films to getting together with friends in the woods to chuck dirt clods directly into one another's eyes, all of which provided me with important skills and insights that remain valuable to this day. Those free hours became the model for how I wanted to live the rest of my life."[3]

Most of us of a certain age remember these hours upon hours of exploration, free time, and hanging out. Sometimes in the afternoon after school, sometimes on a Saturday morning or a Sunday afternoon.

But in our current culture, the idea of "play" is a lost art.

Children intuitively value the power and importance of play. They are able to entertain themselves, engage with the world, and find joy wherever they are, whatever the circumstances. Somewhere along the line, however, that ability gets bleached out of us, and adults find themselves feeling obligated to "be mature" and to "take things more seriously." Certainly, this is valuable conditioning in terms of becoming a functioning member of society, and as adults, our behavior must, of course, be appropriate for our surroundings, but are we sacrificing a sense of awe and wonder in our lives in the name of maturity and decorum?

Unstructured time to experiment, explore, wander around, think, and just goof off is a necessary part of life because it gives us a chance to experiment, reflect, and decompress. And a lack of opportunity to play comes at a cost. This is not just for adults who feel that the concept of play is for kids ("I can't just goof off or wander around; I have too many responsibilities."), but sadly, even for our children. As Krieder says later in that same paragraph, "Even *children* are busy now, scheduled down to the half-hour with classes and extracurricular activities. They come home at the end of the day as tired as grown-ups." In the name of education and advancement, I have watched my own daughters drop into their beds in tears at 10:00 or 11:00 p.m., having slaved over textbooks and worksheets and homework since they got home from school, with only a break for dinner, no time for play at all.

How can we, as adults, reintroduce the idea of play into our lives? Here are just a few ideas:

- Fly a kite in the park.
- Ride a bike.
- Take a Segway tour near the bay.
- Take a walk in the woods for no reason.
- Look for shells along the beach.
- Write a poem or a song.
- Tell a joke.
- Wade in a stream.
- Paint a picture.
- Make a drawing.

- Collect rocks or leaves as we wander through our neighborhood with no agenda or purpose but just to explore life.

Sometimes society takes small steps in the right direction. Not too long ago, for example, adult coloring books burst on the scene and were all the rage. I understand the attraction. Coloring is something that, as children, we found fun, comforting, and soothing. As adults, we call it "therapeutic," and it is. The bottom line is that it makes us feel good because it's creative, there isn't a purpose based on our responsibilities or obligations, and as a bonus, it reminds us of a simpler time.

By the time you read this, that fad may have become passé. But how many *other* activities from our childhood could we think of that would give us that same sense of comfort, joy, and abandon we had as kids, going through our box of sixty-four Crayolas (The one with the sharpener on the side, of course!) and scribbling in our coloring books, all over a horsey or a giant set of alphabetized blocks?

As a teacher, you can also develop a sense of play inside your classroom walls. You can infuse your lessons with the same kind of joy and abandon and exploration that you had as your friends and you rode your bikes all over the neighborhood. Think about it: Sometimes you had a destination and sometimes you didn't. Sometimes you said, "Let's just see what happens if we do this and go there." This approach is particularly important for us to remember while juggling increasing duties, complex standards, and relentless standardized testing.

What if you did that now and then with your lessons? What if, every so often, you just had a basic structure or beginning and an ending, and like a jazz musician, you riffed, explored, experimented, and improvised in the middle just to see what would happen, what it would sound like, and where you would end up? Even if that sounds risky, think about how, much like play, that sense of abandon would liberate and excite you, and by extension, your students.

Play has value all its own.

Sanctuaries

The thing we forget, as adults with obligations and responsibilities that exist outside of the sandbox we knew as toddlers or the bike rides we knew as tweens or teens, is that play has value all its own. It gives our life color, texture, and nuance that gives us a greater sense of depth and fulfillment as we navigate our days.

I once belonged to a wedding party where the bride, bridesmaids, and an entourage of helpers, handlers, make-up artists, photographers, and videographers prepared for the event in a large room behind the church altar. The groom and all of the groomsmen, however, were asked to cool their heels in the much smaller, less well-appointed church music room while they waited for the ceremony to begin. The room was serviceable and pleasant, and the company was good, so I didn't mind too much. And when it comes right down to it, the wedding, as we all know, is not about the groom, anyway. Nevertheless, there wasn't much to do as we waited for our cue.

I suppose men get bored pretty easily because it wasn't too long before one of us noticed that on top of the wooden rack of choir robes sat a stack of straw hats—the kind you would see being worn by a barbershop quartet. Another one of us found a set of bongo drums in the corner. A third groomsman (It might have been me; this was more than twenty years ago, and memory fades. Okay, it was me.) somehow managed to scare up a kazoo.

Before you can say, "Sweet Adelaide," one groomsman started beating on the bongos, I started blowing on the kazoo, and the entire male wedding party grabbed the straw hats and began dancing around the room in a giant circle, performing a spontaneous interpretative dance that was both fun and, yet, out of context, would have been a bizarre spectacle to anyone who witnessed it.

As it turned out, someone did witness it. Not long after we started, the bride's brother came in and jokingly said to the groom, "Do you know how much it's going to cost you for me *not* to mention this to your soon-to-be wife?"

Okay, I was the groom.

If there is room for an interpretative dance with bongo drums, straw hats, and a kazoo at a wedding, even when it's your own, maybe we are missing out on other opportunities for play in our lives that just might put smiles on our faces and make our lives a little more lively and fun.

In his article "Reclaiming the Power of Play," writer Stephen T. Asma breaks the concept of play into two parts—active and passive. He suggests that the passive types of play "anesthetize" us and require no real engagement; they come, he says, with no "effort, skill, or struggle."[4] Passive play might include something like vegging out in front of the television (where, I confess, too many of my life's hours have been spent). Active play, on the other hand, has a cost. You must practice a skill, create something (write, sculpt, paint), or expend some energy (work out at the gym, take a walk, go whitewater rafting). As Asma suggests, the great thing is that, during play, we are not measuring ourselves in terms of our productivity (If I can only write six more poems before 5:00 p.m., I can clock out.), but that play has its own rewards.

In the film *Dead Poet's Society*, John Keating, an inspirational teaching role model of mine played by the inimitable Robin Williams, tells his young charges, "Medicine, law, business, engineering—these are noble pursuits and necessary to sustain life. But poetry, beauty, romance, love—these are what we stay alive for."[5]

He could have just as easily added the idea of play.

By its very nature and definition, play is impractical. It is often without purpose. It can be whimsical. And when I look around, I can tell you that in this, the first third of the twenty-first century, whimsy is sorely lacking in most of our lives.

Starting today, let's allow more impracticality, more purposelessness, more whimsy into our world.

Let's re-learn how to play.

Even as adults—maybe *especially* as adults—we must reclaim our sense of play. It's crucial. Not as a practical matter that will help us build a muscle so that we can be better at more serious, formal, or "important" endeavors. No. We must indulge in it simply for its own sake—as a form of exploration, as an attempt at adventure and spontaneity, as a respite from the thousand other "must dos" and "need to dos" and "have to dos" that take up our all-too-finite amount of time on this planet.

Each of us has moments in our lives and opportunities in our circumstances to play—to find the joy, humor, entertainment, and peace in any given situation. It takes practice to recognize it, but it's there. The challenge for you, then, is to isolate those moments and immerse yourself in a sense of fun, frivolity, and festivity. Not all the time, of course, but when you feel you need it and when it will fill your heart and fulfill your spirit.

No matter what is going on, just remember that you can always do what those groomsmen and I did while waiting for that solemn event to begin.

You can simply grab a hat and dance.

My Sanctuary Plan
Pamper Triggers, Bliss Stations, Soul Food, and Play

Pamper Triggers

My Pamper Triggers include:

1. _____
2. _____
3. _____
4. _____
5. _____

Bliss Station

My ideal Bliss Station looks like:

_____

_____

_____

PLAY

Three ways I can include a greater sense of play in my life include:

1. _____
2. _____
3. _____

Three types of play I can incorporate back into my life:

1._____

2._____

3._____

Saying Yes

Once you've said no to the extra or excessive obligations and responsibilities—that you know are not in alignment with your values, that will overextend you, and that will not allow you to do your best work—then it's time to learn how to say yes.

But what do you say yes *to*?

You say yes to the things that make your heart leap.

You say yes to the things that fulfill your soul, renew your spirit, and give you the greatest and deepest satisfaction.

The funny thing is: You know *exactly* what those things are. You've always known. The trouble is that you probably haven't allowed yourself to pursue them, wallow in them, luxuriate in them, or revel in them because you've filled your life with the things that you feel you *must* do, that you are *required* to do, that you feel *obligated* to do because others have asked or made you feel guilty for *not* doing them.

This doesn't mean that everything is always fun and games. Sometimes, of course, it is necessary to do things that you don't want to do. That's true for everyone. And even within the things that we love, there are duties and obligations that are less than fulfilling, that are difficult, that are even inherently unpleasant.

You may feel profoundly fulfilled, for example, by the deep love and satisfaction you get from having a pet. My family loves our animals. In owning them, we have said yes to something that fulfills us. Even so, we must clean

Sanctuaries

up after our dog, Brad Pitt (It's my dog; I'll name him whatever I want.), when he does his business in the yard. And when our cat, George Clooney, barfs on my bathrobe in the middle of the night, I have to throw it in the washing machine (the robe, not the cat, just to be clear. . .). Things aren't always rosy and fun with pets, but overall, we are working in harmony with elements of life that fulfill us, and we are saying yes to the things that give us the greatest joy. We have made a decision to choose something that is in alignment with our most authentic selves.

I'd hazard a guess that most people, perhaps even you, do not say yes nearly enough to things that fulfill them. If that's you, you may wonder why you are walking through this world with this vague feeling of unease and dissatisfaction.

Poet E. E. Cummings once said, "I imagine that yes is the only living thing."[6] What he's saying is that the right yes is a living thing, and it helps make us more alive when we embrace and accept our truest yes response. If you've ever said yes to something that was in total alignment with your value system, your interests, your skills and gifts, and your passions, then you know what he means. Saying the right kind of yes can be one incredibly organic, totally natural path to happiness and contentment.

Once you've removed the unnecessary, extra, or excessive elements from your calendar, your life, and your mind, start looking around for the things that fuel your contentment. Keep an eye open—in fact, actively pursue—those things that light you up.

When you find it, say . . .

Yes. This lights me up.

Yes. This makes me come alive.

Yes. This gives me a sense of peace.

Yes. This gives me a feeling of connection.

Yes. I am passionate about this, and it gives me a tremendous sense of satisfaction and fulfillment.

Yes. This gives me a sense of happiness and contentment.

What can you say yes to? What about . . .

- The vacation you've always wanted to take to New York City

- Working out
- Taking Saturdays off just for you
- Eating healthier
- Writing that book you've always wanted to write
- Starting that side business
- Exploring that new relationship
- Letting go of guilt, shame, or resentment
- Forgiving those who have wronged you (for your peace, not theirs)

Derek Sivers, creator of the online music store CD Baby and author of *Anything You Want: 40 Lessons for the New Kind of Entrepreneur*, says "If you're not saying, 'Hell, yeah!' about something, say no."[7]

Elizabeth Gilbert, author of *Eat, Pray, Love* and *Big Magic*, says when you find something that your intuition is repelling against, you need to give yourself permission to say, "Not this." By the same token, once you have done that, you must have the courage and strength to be open to the things that make your heart sing and say yes.

And then say yes again.
Say yes.
Yes.
Yes.
And then say, "Yes. This is what I want."
This.
This.
This.

Saying No

What is possibly the only thing more important than saying yes?
That's easy.
Saying no.
Anne Lamott, a writer whose overarching themes include faith and self-care, has famously said that "no is a complete sentence."
And she's right.
But that doesn't mean it's a simple or easy thing to do.
It is extremely challenging to say "no" in the face of nearly constant demands on our time, energy, and focus. No one likes the idea that we are disappointing the people we care about so we often agree to things that we know in our hearts and minds are more than we should take on.
Of course, it's no news flash that teachers are notorious overachievers and endless givers. Because they love and care about their students and want them to do the best job possible, many educators have a difficult time knowing when to set boundaries. And the system doesn't really help them know when it's all right to step back, take a breath, and elect not to participate in an activity, a committee, or any other kind of new responsibility. In fact, it seems the system is often only too happy to bleed them, use them up, and take all they have to give.
That means it's up to the teachers themselves to put up a hand—I'm envisioning Diana Ross or one of the Supremes doing the choreography for "Stop! In the Name of Love" here—and say, "No, I can't do this right now."

Once, during a workshop I was giving for a group of teachers in New Jersey, I got to the part where I talked about learning how to politely and gracefully say no so that they don't overextend themselves and add to their sense of being overwhelmed and burned out.

During this segment of the presentation, I had the participants follow me in a choral response with the following statement: "I don't have to do it all," and then I said, "Repeat after me," and they did. And then I said, "Okay, let's stop the sentence just before the word *all*. Repeat after me: I don't have to do it."

And they repeated.

This exercise was very uncomfortable for some of them.

But they weren't the only ones for whom it was uncomfortable.

After the presentation, I was chatting with an administrator about my talk, and he said that while he greatly enjoyed it, there was one part that made him nervous.

"That part where you told them that they don't have to do it all. That's what I'm afraid of. What if they all listened to you? What if *everyone* said that? If all of my teachers said no, then nothing would get done."

I understand the administrator's point. I really do.

But let's take a moment to unpack a couple of things here.

First of all, that administrator was coming from a place of fear and anxiety, a place of scarcity. What if no one will coach soccer or be the cheer advisor? What if I don't have enough people to be on the accreditation committee or to chaperone the dance? What if no teacher steps up to be the PTSA teacher representative? The problem is that fear often clouds our perception and keeps us from seeing simple, and completely manageable, solutions to problems when they arise.

Secondly, I am not suggesting anarchy, mutiny, or revolution. Any time you encourage "the masses" to go against the prevailing system in any way, the people running that system get a little antsy. I get that. But I'm not saying you should *always* say no. What I'm suggesting is that you stay in tune with your own sense of self and know what you are and ARE NOT capable of. Know when you should set a limit or a boundary. Know when saying "no" is not only absolutely the best choice you can be making for yourself but also ensures that when you *do* commit to a new responsibility, you are fresh and can do your best work. The sad truth is, schools are often all too happy to accept a teacher on a committee, who has an overwhelming number of other plates spinning in the air and is barely hanging on, because at least they found their new committee member.

Think of it like a choir: Everyone is singing, and the sound is beautiful. But it's understood that, every now and then, someone must take a breath. And when that person takes a breath, everyone else keeps singing, and the music keeps going. When that person is singing again, someone else gets to take a breath, and the music keeps going. And so on.

It's not selfish for that person to take a breath; it's a necessity if that person is to return to the song in full force.

Finally, to assuage the sense of fear and scarcity, we need to operate from a place of faith and trust. We need to trust, for example, that someone *will* step up to coach soccer or be the cheer advisor. We need to have faith that there are enough people on any given staff that, when a need arises, someone will be in a calm and relaxed enough state to help out and do what needs to be done. The hard part, though, is recognizing that if no one is able to step up because everyone is overworked, overburdened, and overscheduled, then maybe we need to do some restructuring of the system itself. And don't think that I don't know how scary that is to everyone. But sometimes it is necessary if you don't want your teachers leaving in droves because they are overworked and burned out. At that point, it's time to ask ourselves what is truly important: a relaxed, enthusiastic teacher who can energetically and passionately serve his or her students for years to come—or another bake sale?

One year our principal pulled me aside and asked me to be a staff leader on our accreditation team. I admired our principal—whom I saw as a man of vision and passion—and I wanted to support him, so I said yes. I knew I had many other obligations going on and that it would mean a serious increase in my workload. And sometimes you have to say yes, even in those situations. I've done it before with great success. In this case, I knew I would also be paired with one of my favorite teachers on campus, another educator whose passion and dedication I greatly admired and with whom I'd never worked. I didn't see how I could say no.

But as soon as we got into the heat of things, I knew I'd made a mistake. I didn't believe in the accreditation system, so leading others transparently and authentically wasn't possible. My other obligations kept me from showing up to the meetings with my partner properly prepared and ready to go, forcing her to do more of the work and carry more of the weight. After realizing that I'd overextended myself, I tried to show up to our meetings with a positive attitude, ready to lead, but it was hard to hide the fact that I wasn't. And when we were done, I was so embarrassed by my "performance" that I took the Barnes and Noble gift card we were given as a thank you from the administration and, as a kind of apology, gave it to my co-leader. I didn't feel I'd earned it.

I promised myself then to make more careful decisions in the future. Saying yes in that situation helped no one, least of all the principal I admired and who needed me. It took a long time to let go of the feeling of guilt that I'd let down two people whose approval meant a great deal to me.

It was a silly waste of everyone's time and energy in hindsight, but I realize now I should have simply said, "No. I can't do this now. It's not for me. I'm sure you'll find someone else who could do it even better than I could."

Learning to say no as a complete sentence takes practice.

Learning to say no as a complete sentence takes practice.

But it is, in fact, a muscle made stronger over time with exercise.

The next time someone asks for a demand on your time or energy, check in with your body, your mind, and your heart, and if you want to be the advisor for the Academic Decathlon team, if that's where your gifts and your passion and your enthusiasms lie, then go for it!

But if you already know that you have too much going on, do both of you a favor and decline as politely and gracefully as you can.

And if you say no, say it with strength and confidence.

But also say it without guilt or regret.
Because the bottom line is that it's okay not to do *everything*.
And if you say no? Just remember:
You're still a good teacher.
You're still a good person.
And you still work hard enough.

---

[1] Brown, Damon. "This is Simon Sinek's Guaranteed Secret to Success Most of Us Won't Do." Inc.com. inc.com/damon-brown/this-is-simon-sineks-guaranteed-secret-to-success-most-of-us-wont-do.html.

[2] Kleon, Austin. "The Bliss Station." Austin Kleon. July 21, 2016. https://austinkleon.com/2016/07/21/the-bliss-station.

[3] Kreider, Tim. "The Busy Trap." *Opinionator*, New York Times. June 30, 2012. opinionator.blogs.nytimes.com/2012/06/30/the-busy-trap.

[4] Asma, Stephen T. "Reclaiming the Power of Play." Opinionator, *New York Times*. April 27, 2015. https://opinionator.blogs.nytimes.com/author/stephen-t-asma.

[5] *Dead Poet's Society*. Directed by Peter Weir. Premiered June 9, 1989.

[6] Cummings, E. E. "Poem #40." *50 Poems*. New York: Grosset & Dunlap,1940.

[7] Sivers, Derek. *Anything You Want: 40 Lessons for a New Kind of Entrepreneur*. New York: Penguin, 2015.

My Sanctuary Plan for Saying Yes and Saying No

Saying Yes

Three things I can say yes to that will improve the quality of my self-care (and life!):

1. _____
2. _____
3. _____

Saying No

Three things I can say no to that will improve the quality of my self-care (and life!):

1. _____
2. _____
3. _____

My Sanctuary Plan to Embrace Self-Care

If you learn nothing else from this book, it is crucial that you understand the power of embracing self-care. To reflect on how you can apply these concepts to your life, please complete the following open-ended statements:

One place I can create a sanctuary is . . .

One time and place I can incorporate silence into my life is . . .

One way I can slow down the pace of my life is . . .

One way I can practice stillness is . . .

One way I can create and embrace space is . . .

One way I can practice serving is . . .

Every time you feel the stress, anxiety, and tension rise in your life, go back to this list and complete these statements.

Give yourself the gift of lower stress and greater self-care.

Resilience

Fall down seven times; get up eight.
—ancient Chinese proverb

In every classroom, there are a number of students who, even though they have come from difficult backgrounds and have had severe challenges in their lives, rise up and deal with those obstacles and challenges with poise and grace and perseverance. Some are hungry, some come from abusive homes, some deal with parents who struggle with alcohol or drug addiction, and some are simply ignored, neglected, or undervalued under their own roofs. And still, they endure, they perform, and they even *succeed*. In many cases, the teachers who know their stories watch this, scratch their heads, and say, "How is that possible?"

These students have, without exception, learned the beauty and the grace of resilience.

According to the American Psychological Association, resilience is "the process of adapting well in the face of adversity, trauma, tragedy, threats or significant sources of stress." It is the gift of performing well when you are faced, as we all are at times, with the unexpected, the tragic, the traumatic, and the stressful.

But learning to be resilient and figuring out how to gracefully bounce back from adversity is also a form of self-care.

Carol Dweck, author of *Mindset: The Psychology of Success*, talks about the distinction between a "fixed" mindset and a "growth" mindset.[1] In a fixed mindset, people's positions and perspectives are often rigid and paralyzed, unable to adapt or change. But people who have what Dweck calls a "growth" mindset are more flexible and able to dance with the adversity they encounter in life, allowing themselves to see new and different possibilities, even in the face of stress and challenge.

Resilience, then, is, at least in part, a function of one's mindset.

Put another way, resilience is both an art *and* a science.

Failure

Let's talk about failure. First of all, talking about this particular subject is a bit of a taboo in our culture. Many of us think that if we talk about failure, we will, in some Karmic way, magnetize more of it in our direction. I often fight against this impulse myself. It's highly unlikely, of course, yet we still avoid this topic, nervous that it will bring more failure hurtling toward us.

You've probably all seen the meme that uses the word "fail" as an acronym for "First Attempt In Learning." We are fond of pointing this out to our students, but do we give ourselves the same grace? Do we allow ourselves mistakes and missteps on the way to success and progress? Not usually. More often, our internal monologue criticizes and judges us if things don't work out the way we intended.

As it happens, failure is not an objective truth; it's a perspective. If something doesn't go the way we want it to go, we can choose to look at it as if we have "failed" and allow that to damage and soil our attitude in a way that creates negative energy around the rest of what we do. Or we can say to ourselves, "Okay, that didn't go the way I wanted it to go," so why didn't it? And what can I learn from this experience that I can use to turn this situation into something more positive?

You can change your mind about the extent and degree of your "failure" then use it as a reflection piece to make things even better.

Adversity and What to Do with It

We all encounter adversity in life—those challenges, obstacles, and bad luck that make us feel that life is difficult, not working in our favor, or downright unpleasant or traumatic.

And sometimes it can be really difficult to know how to cope with adversity. We may struggle to figure out answers to our questions or solutions to our problems. We gnash our teeth about how to file something away or let something go.

But there are skills and techniques that help us build our sense of resilience in the face of life's adversities.

I once had a communication teacher in college who taught us about the fight-or-flight response. After describing how, when we encounter adversity, we may sometimes run away or sometimes stay and fight, he pointed out that there is a third approach. It was neither fight *nor* flight, but in fact, to split the difference between the two, one where you just stood your ground, stayed calm, and just did what you needed to do.

His model looked like this:

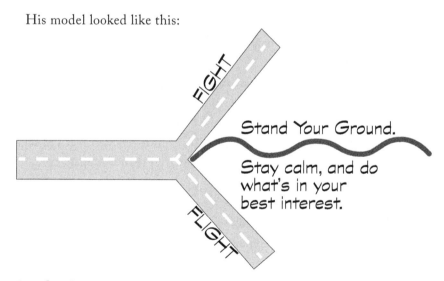

Tips for Resilience

1. Get enough sleep and/or rest—This allows your head to be clear so you can think straight and make proper judgments. Lack of rest impairs our judgment and decision-making process.

2. Cultivate a vibrant social system—When a student is upset, and I'm worried about him or her, my first question is always, "Do you have

people to talk to?" and when they say yes, I say, "Tell me three people." And if they have trouble coming up with a third one, I tell them to add me to the list.

3. **Face things**—Avoid avoidance.
4. **Identify opportunities**—Look for the good.
5. **Recharge and recover**—Schedule it. Don't wait for it to happen randomly or serendipitously.

To be sure, it can run much deeper than this, and if you find yourself in a deep depression or sense of hopelessness, it is my sincere desire that you will seek professional help. But for those run-of-the-mill, everyday adversities that everyone encounters, please don't discount the potential of one of the approaches listed above to make a significant positive difference and get you back on track. Don't forget that there are also books, articles, and online resources you can explore to help you combat the challenges and ultimately improve your resilience.

When you are faced with adversity and are attempting to bounce back or, at the very least, attempting to endure or persevere, try focusing on what you have and what is within your control. Use "I am" affirmations to reprogram the internal tape loop that, as mine once did, is more likely to say, "I'm such an idiot," than to say something like, "I am smarter than this challenge, and I will figure out a solution."

It's very important, when attempting to practice resiliency, to learn to treat yourself as you would treat someone you love because, if you're not there already, eventually you will become someone you love.

Another approach is to remember these two words: *everything* and *nothing*.

Everything is temporary, and nothing is insurmountable.

As in, *everything* is temporary, and *nothing* is insurmountable.

Put another way, no challenge you encounter will last forever; they are all temporary. And nothing you experience is insurmountable. There is a way out of (or at least a way to cope with) any adversity you encounter. Remembering the words *everything* and *nothing* can help you carry on through the typical tribulations you will encounter in life.

And learning these methods of coping is most certainly a fundamental type of self-care.

Standing your ground, staying calm, and doing what's in your best interests—despite the stimulus coming at you—is, in part, what resilience looks like. When it comes right down to it, all of life is a lesson, and some of those lessons can be harrowing, intimidating, or just plain painful. One thing to keep in mind is that often suffering (or what we might *perceive* as an adversity) is really just a thwarted expectation—in other words, we are experiencing what we call a challenge or an adversity simply because we didn't get what we wanted. But if you increase your capacity to accept what "is," then the amount of "suffering" can be greatly reduced. And learning to reduce the amount and degree of your suffering is a form of resilience.

Resilience is not a trait so much as it is a way of approaching life, a brightly colored thread or ribbon that unfolds as your life progresses. It's not so much about how you respond to a challenge today but how your total outlook allows you to cope with the upheaval that life inevitably throws at you over time. And learning to persist through life's storms can only increase one's sense of hope and equanimity.

Resilience, then, is not a quality of the lucky few but a skill we all can learn in order to not only survive, but thrive, in the classroom. And as a bonus, in life.

---

[1] Dweck, Carol S. *Mindset: The Psychology of Success.* New York: Ballantine Books, 2007.

What's Next

Life can be hard.

Along with daily personal issues, anxieties, and stressors, we must also cope with divisive politics, global tragedies, and now, even violence in the schools in the form of random and unpredictable school shootings (a trend I deeply pray has run its course by the time you're reading this). And when you combine all of that with the seemingly endless responsibilities that are heaped upon a teacher's plate by various administration, district, and state mandates—all with the understanding that we will somehow just "make it work"—it often seems that the stress is constant and relentless. Sometimes we want to hide beneath our desks and never come out. Okay, maybe that's just me, but you get my point. It often seems like so much of it is beyond our control and out of our circle of influence.

The good news, though, is that you can improve it.

There are certain things that you can control.

You have more power than you think to affect massive improvements, both in how you live as you teach *and* how you function outside the four walls of your classroom.

The key is to focus on those things that are within your power to change and make a plan.

Learning to include a self-care component in your teaching practice is a four-step process:

Permission—You must give yourself permission to take care of yourself and feel that it is okay. Jettison guilt.

Action—You must take specific action to move the needle forward and make sure your self-care occurs.

Grace—You must learn to forgive yourself when you stumble and when things don't go the way you expect. Remember: It's a path and a journey, not a competition. There is no finish line.

Success—Learn to identify, internalize, and celebrate your personal success along the way. You'll be glad you did.

I hope *Sanctuaries: Self Care Secrets for Stressed Out Teachers* has shown you the path toward making some mindset shifts that will allow you greater freedom in your life to take care of YOU. I also hope it has given you some concrete tools and actionable strategies for improving the quality of your self-care and teaching you how to maximize your performance without sacrificing yourself.

If you're feeling stressed or anxious in your life, I urge you to reflect on, and then apply, some of the concepts found in this book and see if you notice a difference, an improvement in the quality of your days.

I wrote *Sanctuaries* because it's important to me that you take care of yourself. Not only because I consider myself a peace and self-care artist for teachers, but because I also think you do the most important work on the planet, and I would like to see you make it through your career in a way that not only sustains, but fulfills, you.

In short, the fact that you are a teacher makes you my hero.

And we need you.

So I want you to take care of yourself.

Starting today.

Let me personally invite you to communicate with me about any of the topics in this book.

There are many ways for you to participate in an ongoing dialogue about your own well-being and The Zen Teacher message:

- Join The Zen Teacher closed Facebook group, which can be found on Facebook by searching "The Zen Teacher Closed Group."
- Email me at teachingzen@gmail.com.
- Find me on Twitter at @thezenteacher.
- Visit my website and read my blog at www.thezenteacher.com.
- Subscribe to my newsletter by filling out the form on my website.

I look forward to hearing from you and continuing our conversation.

Peace and Love,

Danny

Acknowledgments

I would like to thank the following people who helped make this book possible. My deepest thanks and heartfelt gratitude are extended to:

Dave and Shelley Burgess, for publishing *Sanctuaries: Self-Care Secrets for Stressed Out Teachers*, putting me on a path I love, and helping me realize a new calling—namely, helping teachers take care of themselves. I am proud to be a DBC, Inc. author.

Genesis Kohler, Mariana Lenox, and Erin Casey, for creating another beautiful artifact that celebrates the words between the covers in a way that makes them art and would have been impossible for me to do by myself.

Michael and Janet Tricarico, my parents, for their constant support, unconditional love, and endless faith.

The West Hills High School English Department, for giving me an opportunity to affect the lives of thousands of students. Not everyone is lucky enough to have a job where they create ripple effects into the future, and I do not take that responsibility lightly.

I would also like to thank the following people for improving the quality of my teaching, my writing, my life, or all three: Tatum Tricarico, Tessa Tricarico, Valerie Christian, Ashley Worth, Rodd Moses, A.J. Acosta, Kristin Amundson McLaughlin, Chrissy Pestolis McDuff, Christopher Morrissey, Geoffrey Anderson, Ed Hollingsworth, Audrey Becker, Terry Theroux, Laura Preble, David Stanley, and Teresa and Joe Shea. And special thanks to Leonard Cohen, Sam Shepard, Edward Albee, Richard Brautigan, David Sedaris, Bob Dylan, and David Mamet for making me want to put my ideas down in words on paper and share them with others, just as you did with me.

And again, this book is for…

Holler.

You are still missed, Lord Holler. Thank you for showing me how this whole teaching thing is done and for often asking (as your uncle reminded us), "Why should we all be miserable?"

Let Dan Tricarico Help Your Staff Avoid Teacher Burnout!

Learn to Maximize Your Performance Without Sacrificing Yourself

Are the ever-increasing demands of the classroom or the front office causing your teachers and administrators to feel overwhelmed, overworked, or overburdened?
Does your staff experience high levels of stress, anxiety, or tension?
Do your colleagues consider burnout not only possible, but inevitable?
It doesn't have to be that way.
Book a Zen Teacher Workshop for your school or district and show your staff that you are interested in their personal well-being, their mental and emotional health, and their improved self-care.

The Zen Teacher Workshop
shows teachers and administrators how to…

- Act with intention
- Accept what is
- Be present in the moment—Focus on The Now
- Show compassion
- Pay attention
- Live mindfully
- Create space
- Reflect and meditate on their practice
- Detach from expectations and embrace the "teachable moment"
- Give themselves the gift of silence and stillness
- Embrace subtraction for a greater sense of fulfillment in the classroom
- Value Self-Care and Self-Compassion

Let me teach your staff the tools and strategies to help them navigate the stressors inherent in the education profession. Educators from around the country have benefited from The Zen Teacher workshop and have implemented the approaches I share in this fun, engaging, interactive workshop that helps educators reduce personal stress and create more calm work environments, resulting in an increased likelihood not only of personal peace, but of teacher and administrator retention.

To request a quote for a Zen Teacher workshop, send an email to teachingzen@gmail.com.

I look forward to hearing from you.

Dan

More from Dave Burgess Consulting, Inc.

Since 2012, DBCI has been publishing books that inspire and equip educators to be their best. For more information on our DBCI titles or to purchase bulk orders for your school, district, or book study, visit **DaveBurgessconsulting.com/DBCIbooks**.

More from the PIRATE™ Series
Teach Like a PIRATE by Dave Burgess
eXPlore Like a Pirate by Michael Matera
Learn Like a Pirate by Paul Solarz
Play Like a Pirate by Quinn Rollins
Run Like a Pirate by Adam Welcome

Lead Like a PIRATE™ Series
Lead Like a PIRATE by Shelley Burgess and Beth Houf
Balance Like a Pirate by Jessica Cabeen, Jessica Johnson, and Sarah Johnson
Lead with Culture by Jay Billy
Lead with Literacy by Mandy Ellis

Leadership & School Culture
Culturize by Jimmy Casas
Escaping the School Leader's Dunk Tank by Rebecca Coda and Rick Jetter
The Innovator's Mindset by George Couros
Kids Deserve It! by Todd Nesloney and Adam Welcome
Let Them Speak by Rebecca Coda and Rick Jetter
The Limitless School by Abe Hege and Adam Dovico
The Pepper Effect by Sean Gaillard
The Principled Principal by Jeffrey Zoul and Anthony McConnell
The Secret Solution by Todd Whitaker, Sam Miller, and Ryan Donlan

Start. Right. Now. by Todd Whitaker, Jeffrey Zoul, and Jimmy Casas
Stop. Right. Now. by Jimmy Casas and Jeffrey Zoul
Unmapped Potential by Julie Hasson and Missy Lennard
Your School Rocks by Ryan McLane and Eric Lowe

Technology & Tools
50 Things You Can Do with Google Classroom by Alice Keeler and Libbi Miller
50 Things to Go Further with Google Classroom by Alice Keeler and Libbi Miller
140 Twitter Tips for Educators by Brad Currie, Billy Krakower, and Scott Rocco
Code Breaker by Brian Aspinall
Google Apps for Littles by Christine Pinto and Alice Keeler
Master the Media by Julie Smith
Shake Up Learning by Kasey Bell
Social LEADia by Jennifer Casa-Todd
Teaching Math with Google Apps by Alice Keeler and Diana Herrington

Teaching Methods & Materials
All 4s and 5s by Andrew Sharos
Ditch That Homework by Matt Miller and Alice Keeler
Ditch That Textbook by Matt Miller
The EduProtocol Field Guide by Marlena Hebern and Jon Corippo
Instant Relevance by Denis Sheeran
LAUNCH by John Spencer and A.J. Juliani
Make Learning MAGICAL by Tisha Richmond
Pure Genius by Don Wettrick
Shift This! by Joy Kirr
Spark Learning by Ramsey Musallam
Sparks in the Dark by Travis Crowder and Todd Nesloney
Table Talk Math by John Stevens
The Classroom Chef by John Stevens and Matt Vaudrey
The Wild Card by Hope and Wade King
The Writing on the Classroom Wall by Steve Wyborney

Inspiration, Professional Growth & Personal Development
4 O'Clock Faculty by Rich Czyz
Be REAL by Tara Martin
Be the One for Kids by Ryan Sheehy
The EduNinja Mindset by Jennifer Burdis
How Much Water do We Have? by Pete and Kris Nunweiler
P Is for Pirate by Dave and Shelley Burgess
The Path to Serendipity by Allyson Aspey
Shattering the Perfect Teacher Myth by Aaron Hogan
Stories from Webb by Todd Nesloney
Talk to Me by Kim Bearden
The Zen Teacher by Dan Tricarico

Children's Books
Dolphins in Trees by Aaron Polansky
The Princes of Serendip by Allyson Apsey

About the Author

Dan Tricarico lives in San Diego, California, and has been a high school English teacher for more than twenty-five years. He is author of *The Zen Teacher: Creating Focus, Simplicity, and Tranquility in the Classroom* and *Sanctuaries: Self-Care Secrets for Stressed Out Teachers*. In his spare time, he enjoys writing fiction, watching movies, listening to music, reading, and staring out of windows. His first love is writing poetry, and he has published many poems both in print and online.

For more ideas on reduced stress and improved self-care or to sign up for The Zen Teacher newsletter, please visit thezenteacher.com.

Made in the USA
Las Vegas, NV
01 October 2021